CASE STUDIES IN

CULTURAL ANTHROPOLOGY

GENERAL EDITORS
George and Louise Spindler
STANFORD UNIVERSITY

THE HOGHEAD
An Industrial Ethnology of the Locomotive Engineer

THE HOGHEAD

An Industrial Ethnology of the
Locomotive Engineer

By

FREDERICK C. GAMST

University of Massachusetts, Boston

HOLT, RINEHART AND WINSTON

NEW YORK   CHICAGO   SAN FRANCISCO   DALLAS

MONTREAL   TORONTO   LONDON   SYDNEY

For Nicole

Cover photo credit: A Hoghead At His Controls On A Time Freight.

Library of Congress Cataloging in Publication Data

Gamst, Frederick C
   The hoghead : an industrial ethnology of the locomotive engineer.

  Case studies in cultural anthropology
  Bibliography: p. 132
    1. Locomotive engineers—United States.
2. Industrial sociology—Case studies. 3. Ethnology—
United States—Case studies. I. Title. II. Series.
HD8039.R322U53   331.7'62527'0973   80-12232

ISBN: 0-03-052636-1

Foreword

ABOUT THE SERIES

These case studies in cultural anthropology are designed to bring to students, in beginning and intermediate courses in the social sciences, insights into the richness and complexity of human life as it is lived in different ways and in different places. They are written by men and women who have lived in the societies they write about, and who are professionally trained as observers and interpreters of human behavior. The authors are also teachers, and in writing their books they have kept the students who will read them foremost in their minds. It is our belief that when an understanding of ways of life very different from one's own is gained, abstractions and generalizations about social structure, cultural values, subsistence techniques, and other universal categories of human social behavior become meaningful.

ABOUT THE BOOK

Fred Gamst brings to this case study a rare combination of expertise and experience. He is a skilled social scientist who possesses an extensive knowledge of railroad operations and related matters. As a railroad employee in engine service (operation of locomotives), he logged six and one-half years on the job, making over 2000 runs and encountering every variety of such service. Since his initial period of employment, he has maintained contact with railroaders in more than one district and has conducted intensive fieldwork both intermittently and during longer periods. True to the anthropological model, he has also conducted fieldwork on railroads in another culture—in this case the Eritrean railroad of Ethiopia.

While railroading is by no means Dr. Gamst's only professional interest (he is author of another case study in this series on the Qemant of Ethiopia), we know from personal observation how intense his interest is. We first met Fred some years ago when, as a new assistant professor at Rice University in Houston, he was sent to pick us up at the Union Passenger Terminal when we arrived there on Santa Fe's *Bluebonnet*. He greeted us with the comment that, "Journeying by train is the only civilized way to travel." A few years later, we had the privilege of riding with Fred to Mexico City on the *Aztec Eagle*. While he took copious notes and many photographs, he filled us in on the myriad railroad operations and procedures along the route. We were astounded at the complexity of railroading!

It is this combination of long-term direct experience as a participant, together with professional anthropological observation and inquiry, and strong personal interest that has made *The Hoghead* possible. The reader is swept up in the action with a feeling of realism and directness that is rare in the literature of anthropology. One learns more about railroading and railroaders ("rails") than one could think possible in a book of such brief compass. But one learns not only about railroading but about anthropology. Fred Gamst interprets what he observes and records from an anthropological viewpoint, using anthropological concepts. This interpretation is orderly and leads to a progressively cumulative understanding of both the phenomena being studied and the discipline that provides the framework for the study. This is the object of any case study and the major purpose of the series in which this study is placed.

The Hoghead is offered as evidence of our continuing attempt as editors of the CASE STUDIES IN CULTURAL ANTHROPOLOGY to bring the focus of our discipline upon institutions and phenomena in our own and other contemporary complex industrial societies.* Though the many significant and well-done studies, some of which are represented in our series, of remote nonliterate societies and their cultures will endure longer than the communities they report on and interpret, anthropology as a discipline cannot rest its case upon these studies. Anthropology is of great potential relevance to the modern world and to the problems and processes of industrial society. This potential must be demonstrated in studies of the kind represented by *The Hoghead*.

ABOUT THE AUTHOR

Frederick C. Gamst is a professor in the anthropology department, as well as Associate Provost for Graduate Studies, at the University of Massachusetts at Boston, Harbor Campus. He received his B.A. "with highest honors" from the University of California at Los Angeles, his Ph.D. from the University of California at Berkeley, and his Diesel Engineer and Fireman Diploma from the International Correspondence Schools. He has done fieldwork in Ethiopia among peasants, foragers, and railroaders. Dr. Gamst has made extensive studies of railroading in the United States in his contribution to the development of industrial ethnology. In this industry he has done ethnological fieldwork, survey research, and documentary analysis for basic and applied ends, both as an academic researcher and as an industrial consultant.

Dr. Gamst has written articles and reviews on agrarian society and on railroading; he has also written *The Qemant: A Pagan-Hebraic Peasantry* (Holt, Rinehart and Winston, 1969), *Peasants in Complex Society* (Holt, Rinehart and Winston, 1974), and has edited *Studies in Cultural Anthropology* (Rice University Studies, 1975), *Ideas of Culture: Sources and Uses,* with Edward Norbeck (Holt, Rinehart and Winston, 1976), and the "Golden Anniversary Special Issue, Industrial Ethnology" of *Anthropological Quarterly* (1977).

GEORGE AND LOUISE SPINDLER
General Editors
Calistoga, California

* A list of case studies in cultural anthropology on various aspects of American society and culture edited by the Spindlers is furnished at the end of this volume.

Preface

The Hoghead is one result of my research in railroading, among railroaders, which was conducted over a considerable period of time. Information for this book was gathered during six and one-half years of employment (May 1955 through December 1961) in railroad engine service. During this period, information from participant observation was obtained along with documents of various kinds for the eventual writing of a monograph on railroad operations. My experience included every variety of engine service over many hundreds of miles of main and branch lines and in a number of yards and terminal areas. Approximately 2000 runs were made.

From 1962 through 1969, contact was maintained with railroaders on the districts of former employment and new contact was made with railroaders on still other districts in the United States. Also an ethnographic survey was made of the Eritrean railroad of Ethiopia as a basis for intensive ethnological fieldwork at a later date. In 1969 I briefly returned to what I call pseudonymously in this book the "Central City and Urbana Railroad" (CC & U) for the purpose of making preliminary arrangements for intensive, long-term ethnological research on operating employees and especially engine service employees of that carrier. From 1970 through 1975 I conducted seasonal ethnological fieldwork among the engine service employees of the CC & U. The seasons included a semester's leave of absence and a sabbatical semester from Rice University and four summers.

In addition to the participant observation of the period of employment and of the period of formal ethnological research in railroading, a lengthy project in survey research was conducted in 1971–1972. A ten-page questionnaire of 224 questions was designed and pre-pretested and then pretested before it was mailed to engine service employees of what are called "groups A, B, and C." Group A consists of 222 active employees of the Western Division of the CC & U. This railroad operating division is the location of most of my railroad employment and formal ethnological research. The questionnaire was mailed to 100 percent of these employees and a total response of 188, or 84.7 percent, was received. For purposes of comparison and control of data, groups B and C were also surveyed. Group B is from a division of a railroad neighboring the CC & U. A random sample of 20 percent of its 246 engine service employees was chosen, that is, 49. A response of 42, or 85.7 percent, was received. Group C consists of the 90 engine service employees of the Eastern Division of the CC & U. A 75 percent sample was selected (67 men) and a response of 65.7 percent, or 44, was received. Some of the results of the questionnaire are found in various sections of the chapters in *The Hoghead*.

Correspondence over the years from railroaders, especially on the CC & U, but from other carriers as well, has constantly provided me with current events and the personal insights of railroaders. Many have sent me documents, and some have even sent photographs of value in my research. Tape recordings were made of formal responses to my specific and general questions and to loosely structured, "natural" conversations among a number of railroaders. During my period of railroad employment and in the time of formal research right through the present, I have also collected all manner of relevant documentary sources, without which an ethnological study of contemporary industry and work is impossible. Some documents are published, for example: rule books; timetables; technical manuals for use of equipment; and instructional, regulating, and investigating publications of many kinds issued by railroads, trade unions, government, and other firms. Unpublished documents include: official correspondence, reports in mimeographed and other forms, railroad operating bulletins and circulars, train orders and operating messages, and sundry other items.

An extensive photographic record has been made consisting of color slides and black and white and color photographs of operations on the CC & U and other carriers. The pictures provide rich illustrative material, as used in this book. Also, in conjunction with my voluminous field notes on coded cards, the pictures help me to recall, reconstruct, and analyze more exactly than would otherwise be the case the ethnographic reality of the field situation in which the notes were recorded. For further information on method see the third section, entitled "Industrial Ethnology," in the first chapter of this book.

In order to protect the privacy of individual employees and members of their families, and of railroad companies and trade unions, all persons, firms, and places are given pseudonyms in this book. *The Hoghead* attempts to present to the reader factual data and analyses of these data having social scientific interest and usefulness. Exact identification of subjects of research is not relevant to these underlying goals. All photographs in the book of scenes from railroading were taken by me in various parts of the country.

Acknowledgments are in order for a large number of people to whom I am grateful for valuable aid in the course of my railroad research. I am especially grateful to the many railroaders whose cooperation and social support made my research possible. I owe a great debt to those railroaders who helped me by discussing and commenting upon aspects of my study. I give special thanks to Christina V. Flanders, who for over ten years read and clipped for my files all items in the Urbana newspapers concerning the CC & U and other railroads. Thanks are also given for her typing the final draft of the manuscript for this book. I also wish to acknowledge the assistance of Elaine O'Toole, who typed the second draft. Harry W. Rhodes, III, developed and printed the photographs used in this book. Hildegarde Von Laue, in the inter-library loan department of our campus library, provided me with numerous uncommon publications necessary for this book. My wife, Marilou, assisted me during the fieldwork, edited and commented upon the manuscript, and furnished all manner of vital support for my railroad research. My daughter, Nicole, was one year of age when the formal fieldwork began in 1970 and has become a knowledgeable (and encouraging) railroad buff during the course of my research and writing. At the age of three, she wanted to become a locomotive engineer. I am grateful to George and Louise Spindler for their customary careful and instructive editing of the manuscript for this book. Of course, I am solely responsible for all presentations and interpretation of information.

I am also grateful to the editors of *Anthropological Quarterly* for their permission to reprint parts of my essay "An Integrating View of the Underlying Premises of an Industrial Ethnology in the United States and Canada," which introduced that journal's Golden Anniversary Special Issue on Industrial Ethnology (volume 50, number 1, 1977). Research leading to this book was in part supported by National Science Foundation Grant GS 3040 and National Institute of Mental Health Grants MH 2183, 01 and 02.

Cohasset, Massachusetts   Frederick C. Gamst
February 1980

Contents

THE HOGHEAD
An Industrial Ethnology of the Locomotive Engineer

Colorado and Southern road crews preparing to take their locomotives to their trains.

1/Introduction

SCOPE OF THE BOOK

The work and lifestyle of the railroader, particularly the locomotive engineer, are occasionally viewed through American folk song and lore. Apart from this, most people, including social scientists, know little about railroaders. Through this book, the reader enters the world of railroaders and learns about the occupation and life of the locomotive engineer and his fellow workers in an exposition of the ethnological (social and cultural anthropological) study of industry. Railroading is not just another industry among many industries; it is a continuing primordial enterprise of the industrial revolution. Beginnings of railroading are caught up with beginnings of the transformation of agrarian Europe, and slightly later the United States, into something never before experienced by man—an industrial society, strongly grasping the geographic environment that it had thoroughly subjugated to its own ends.

This book provides an in-depth examination of an economically vital occupational role within an industrial setting largely closed to public scrutiny. It develops a vivid account of the nature of work in an industrial urban society. The rhythm and meaning of work tasks are presented in a way that allows the reader to share in and appreciate the concerns, frustrations, and satisfactions of the locomotive engineer at and away from the job. Both ideal and actual patterns of behavior are included in the presentation. Reactions and accommodations of the engineer to the demands of a demanding craft in a fast-paced setting of work are offered to the reader from the customary ethnological depiction of the insider's (here railroader's) point of view.

Technologically engendered restraints upon tasks and upon social relations at work, and extending beyond the job to the home, are discussed in light of controls such as time and mechanical devices, whose requisites cannot be ignored. Injury and death are often the penalties for improper or misjudged compliance with the temporal and mechanical demands of railroading. As the reader will learn, if a train does not vacate a particular stretch of track at a given time according to the complex operating rules, it could find itself occupying the same physical space with another train having authority to occupy the same track at the same time. Similarly, if an engineer does not use his controls in an exacting sequence with correct adjustments of compressed air pressure and amperage in his various braking systems, he could have a "runaway" train wreck. Tragic aftermaths of both kinds of accidents are well known in folklore and in the news media. Emotions of an engineer are shared, from the anxieties of possibly being labeled a "flat wheel" to the minor triumph of waiting and resting in the siding after running along the main line under difficult circumstances.

The reader, through this book, will appreciate somewhat the technical intricacies of the interfacing of man and machine into one dynamic system of production, so vital for the maintenance of an industrial society. Among the knowledge shared by the reader with the engineer are insights into the (mal)functioning of a diesel-electric locomotive, the running of a heavy difficult train down a mountain grade, and the logical coordination of train movements by the seemingly arcane knowledge of operating timetables and train orders. Finally, in this book, social and economic pressures from the larger society encompassing the railroader and his work and home are examined, without which a true understanding of the status of the locomotive engineer is incomplete.

An additional dimension of this study is the discussion of ethnological methods in the third section of this chapter. There the reader learns, as a frame for the book, methods used in obtaining and analyzing information on work, occupation, and industrial organization. These methods allow presentation to the reader of first-hand data gathered largely through sustained direct contact with the subjects of research, "hogheads" and other "rails" in their natural setting.

The second, following, section of this chapter allows the reader to visit briefly what I call the "rail world" and to see things from the customary ethnological perspective, the native viewpoint. This viewpoint could be that of Navajo tribesmen or Portland longshoremen (cf. Downs 1971; Pilcher 1972), but in this case focuses on the enginemen on the "Central City and Urbana Railroad" (CC & U). The names of all railroads, railroad sites, trains, and railroaders used by me in this book are pseudonyms employed to protect the identities of persons and the confidentiality of information I obtained during ethnological fieldwork on the "CC & U" and other railroads. Certain identifying numbers and features have been changed, for example, some rule numbers, locomotive and train numbers, and exact mileages.

Built around the turn of the century, the CC & U was one of the later "transcontinental" railroads spanning the western United States. After a few decades of independent operation, it was included in the "Overland and Western Railway System" (O & W). In recent years, the O & W has reorganized itself so that railroad operations are but one company in a multicompany conglomerate enterprise, the Overland and Western Corporation, which invests heavily in nonrailroad enterprise. The CC & U is divided into two standard railroad operating districts called *divisions*—the Western Division and the Eastern Division—each of which comprises about one-half of the approximately 1000 miles of main line. Each of the two divisions also comprises a seniority district for engine service employees. As is common practice, the CC

& U operates over the track of (four) other railroads and its employees are also governed by, and examined on, the various regulations of these railroads.

In the rail world the locomotive engineer is usually referred to and called a "hoghead" or a "hogger." The words are derived from a particular kind of steam locomotive, introduced in the nineteenth century, which railroaders called a "hog." * Locomotive engineers, locomotive firemen, and hostlers (those who handle and deliver locomotives at servicing sites and in terminal areas) are known collectively as engine service employees, as opposed to train and yard service employees. The former includes brakemen and conductors in freight or passenger service outside of terminal areas, and the latter includes switchmen and switchtenders in switching service inside the terminal. This book follows the practice of some railroads of using synonymously "engine service employees" and "enginemen." Engine, train, and yard service and certain other employees, collectively, are generally known in railroading as "ops" (operating personnel) as opposed to "non-ops" (maintenance, supply, and other support personnel). The operating personnel refer to themselves as "rails." The immediate social setting at work for the hoghead is one of fellow rails.

In order to acquaint the reader with the rail world, we begin a morning's work with one hoghead, M.C. "Clint" Johnson, who has been railroading out of Urbana for thirty-six years. None of the events we experience with him this particular morning are in any way out of the ordinary. The behavior of operating railroaders is structured by an exceedingly large number of detailed operating, mechanical, and other rules formally codified and published by the railroads. These rules will be discussed throughout this book. In the following section, some of the rules will be cited by code number as they direct Johnson's thoughts and acts this particular morning. The citation of rule numbers allows the reader to begin to perceive some of the salient formal elements of organization of the native railroader's viewpoint. Some of the rules are no longer consciously reflected upon by Johnson and his fellow railroaders, but are instead acted upon reflexively. Many rules are part of a rail's basic personality on and off the railroad, for example the rules regarding time (Cottrell 1939, 1940; Kemnitzer 1977). For ease of classification, the rules are prefixed as follows: OR (operating rules), MR (mechanical and air brake rules), AR (agreement—contractual—rules between the railroad and the labor union), TR (timetable and special rules), LR (locomotive-operators' manual regulations, not numbered), and BR (bulletins, circulars, and notices placed by the proper authority in special "bulletin books" to be read before going on duty).

---

*All words in the argot (slang) of railroaders of English-speaking North America will be placed in quotation marks when they are first used in this book (e.g., "hog"), and all technical terms from railroading will be italicized when first used (e.g., *ballast*). Both kinds of words will be explained when introduced and will be listed in the Glossary at the end of this book. Occupational argot, comprised of words and phrases not used in standard English, is the result of a need for terse, efficient communication in an industry such as railroading. Language of this kind usually forms a barrier to communication with outsiders about the occupation and industry. (For additional information on rail argot see Beebe 1938:219–225; Cottrell and Montgomery 1943; Hubbard 1945; Kemnitzer 1973; and Beck 1978.)

IN THE RAIL WORLD

The stars were disappearing from the early dawn sky as the hoghead climbed out of his auto, picked up his well-filled grip, and walked across the employees' parking lot to the small building housing the register and locker rooms for enginemen. Just beyond the building loomed the brightly illuminated engine house, a cavernous structure in which men labored through the night to repair and service the "company's" diesel—electric locomotive units. The railroad never slept or took a holiday; its activities were ceaseless—the work in the shops, the bustle of switch locomotives in the terminal area, and the movement of freight and passenger trains between terminals were without beginning and without end. The air held the sharp smell of diesel exhaust, and the heavy rumble of the units could be heard and felt as they were moved about the servicing area surrounding the engine house.

The hoghead noted with satisfaction the set of units which were waiting for him on the outbound track next to the engine house: four of the new ones, each weighing 185 tons and producing 3600 horsepower. A new unit cost "the company," as the railroad was referred to, about $700,000. The 907 was the lead unit. He did not reflect upon his sense of satisfaction. It was by now a fundamental part of his personality, partially molded by the agreement, or contract, between the company and the Brotherhood of Locomotive Engineers. The high horsepower would move him over the road with dispatch—he was paid by the mile—and the heavy weight of his locomotive meant that he would receive a greater rate of pay per mile (AR 2,8,25). The newness of the units would result in less mechanical trouble "on the road." The four 900s were fresh from the washing facility and emitted the sweet smell of petroleum distillates used as cleaning agents to remove grease and dirt.

Stepping into the bright lights of the register room, the hoghead nodded to another locomotive engineer who was registering off duty, greeting the man with his first real words of the day. The hoghead's earlier, affirmative, sleepy grunts over the telephone did not count as words when at 4:00 A.M. he acknowledged the call of the crew dispatcher (OR 702, 702A, 702B).

"Johnson, take a call for the FCF [Fast Chicago Forwarder] called for 5:30 [A.M.]. Have you got that? Slim Rogers will follow you out of town. I'm calling him for a drag east at 6:00." Johnson had just missed being called for a train of 120 empty cars which would crawl over the grades at 10 m.p.h. Too bad for Slim.

Johnson checked his railroad watch against the master clock on the wall (OR 1,2,3,3A,3C,3E). He read in the various bulletin books the latest bulletins (OR 109) governing operating procedures and conditions on the district over which he would run this morning. He would have to watch for "gandy dancers," track workers, along two stretches of main line being refurbished; the passing track at Randolph was blocked with cars and out of service; and "Fourth paragraph, Rule 82, Form 3000-A Std. Air Brake Rules, is cancelled." Next, he filled in the blanks beside the printed words in the register book: TRAIN "Xtra 907 East," ENGINEER "M.C. Johnson," ON DUTY

"5:30 A," COMPARED WATCH "5:30 A," HOURS RESTED "18," LAT-EST BULLETIN NUMBER "46," FIREMAN "----". He did not complete this last blank. The few firemen who remained were newly hired men and women who were training as engineers, and the hoghead would not have one this trip, as had most often been the case for several years now.

The other engineer said, "Clint, that work train should be out spreading *ballast* [track gravel] three miles east of Piedmont by the time you get there."

"I'll be watching for their flagman," (OR 99E) the hoghead replied. "I'll have a *train order* [telegraphic message from the train dispatcher on a tissue paper form] on them (OR 200-220c, S-H, D-H), but no sense getting up any speed on the two curves out of Piedmont until I see them."

Johnson went over in his head the possible points of meeting the work train. The hoghead knew over 500 miles of main and branch lines of the Western Division "like the palm of my hand." Mark Twain's Mississippi riverboat pilots were not as familiar with their territory.

The head [end of the train] brakeman who would share the cab of the 907 with Johnson came in with the initial train orders and the train dispatcher's clearance form allowing X907 East to enter and move upon the main line (OR 96,97). The hoghead studied the orders. One order had not been expected. The yellow tissue of the "Form 19" crinkled as he held it and read: "ALL TRAINS MUST NOT EXCEED 20 MPH BETWEEN M.P. 23.75 AND M.P. 24 BETWEEN LOGANDALE JCT AND PRENTICE. YELLOW AND GREEN [trackside] SIGNALS NOT DISPLAYED. MADE COM-PLETE AT 304A, HENDERSON [telegraph] OPERATOR." Something must have just happened to undermine the stability of the track at that point, he thought. The hoghead folded his orders carefully, picked up his grip, and headed for the murmuring 907 and its three sisters. In order to reduce delay, and possible extra pay, at the initial terminal, the company no longer wanted him to take the time to inspect a locomotive. Nevertheless, he glanced along the sides of the four units, saw that the air brakes were applied and presumably operative, climbed up onto the lead unit, and entered the cab while the head brakeman released the mandatory handbrake set on the unit. The conductor and rear brakie would be picked up later.

The crew of a train (operating over the road) or of a switch locomotive (operating in yards, main and branch lines, and industrial tracks in terminal areas, such as Urbana or Central City) consists of an engine crew and a ground crew (often confusingly called the "train crew"). The engine crew was traditionally an engineer and his fireman-helper, but most of these crews no longer have a second engine service employee assisting the engineer. The ground crew contains the employee with paramount operating authority over both crews—the conductor. He is in charge of passenger, freight, and terminal/yard runs, coordinates and supervises the work of his ground and engine crews, and is responsible for completion of work assignments such as switching cars for an industry or getting a freight train over the road on schedule. As we shall see, his authority over the engineer is sometimes more a formal operating rule than actual practice. Additionally, the ground crew has from

TABLE 1. CC & U STATIONS*

Weyburn	Crofts (Yard)	Central City Yard
Applegate	JN Tower	Central City
Clover	Hendricks	(32 stations)
Oxford	Dry River (Yard)	Williams (Yard)
(2 stations)	Breeze	(5 stations)
Randolph	Sims	Lewis
(2 stations)	Stone Creek	(5 stations)
Morgan	Golden	Crestview
Prentice	Ridge	(6 stations)
Logandale Jct.	Cementon	Topaz (Yard)
Monroe Jct.	Windsor	(12 stations)
(3 stations)	Westerly	Reed
East Urbana	Mystic	(3 stations)
Urbana Yard	Apex	Acme
(2 stations)	Maxwell	(4 stations)
River Yard	(4 stations)	Jackson (Yard)
Urbana	Piedmont (Yard)	(15 stations)
WN Tower	Locust	Zenith
(3 stations)	Groveton (Yard)	(5 stations)
Kingston	Evergreen	Orwell (Yard)
(3 stations)	Union Tower	(5 stations)
Deep Water Yard	Union City	Cross
Deep Water	Weyburn	(5 stations)
		Crofts (Yard)

*Stations of the CC & U not mentioned by name in this book are not named above. Reading upward and beginning with the left-hand column, one progresses from west to east.

one to three brakemen if in road service or switchmen if in terminal/yard service. The functions of brakemen and switchmen are the same, but the proportions of their tasks usually differ. Usually brakemen ride and serve as lookouts more often and switchmen are more often on the ground throwing track switches, coupling and uncoupling cars and their air hoses, switching cars from track to track while sorting them out, and spotting (positioning) them at their delivery sites, for example a warehouse door, and so forth. On some railroads the terminal/yard conductor is titled an "engine foreman," that is of the switch locomotive and its engine- and groundmen. In the jesting banter of enginemen, it is said that the definition of a full crew is a hoghead, a bakehead (fireman), a swellhead, and several knuckleheads. Brakemen and switchmen retort by saying that when a new brakeman was sent up on the locomotive by the conductor to get a "dummy" (a special air hose), he came back to the caboose leading the hoghead by the hand. Enginemen call the caboose the "ape cage."

A hostler and his helper rolled by with four passenger units on an adjacent engine house track, finishing their night's round of servicing and moving locomotives from "stall" to stall in the "barn" (the engine house). Jim Ryan, the hostler, was much further down the engineer's seniority list than Johnson.

View from engineer's workspace of switchman giving "easy" sign with outstretched arms, second switchman reading switch list, of cars, and yard conductor waiting to guide coupling to car at place where he stands. A tank car is immediately ahead of the locomotive and is being coupled to the boxcar.

He waved at Clint. About ten years from now Jim's seniority would advance enough so that he too could work in the pool of through-freight engineers. By then Clint would be in passenger service "if there are any passenger trains left when I have the seniority to hold a passenger run," the hoghead had once said in the register room. The hoghead attached his train orders to the clip-board provided for the purpose and dropped next to his seat his grip laden with railroad operating rule books and timetables, tools, food, fresh clothing, and toilet articles. He then sat in the padded, pedestal-mounted seat next to the controls and indicator gauges and lights (see page 8). (Through-freight trains run through/ past terminals; such as Urbana, Crofts, Jackson, Williams, and Central City whereas local, or way, freights run part way—or sometimes all the way—between two terminals or else on branch lines. For example, Clint's FCF will "run through" to Chicago.)

He flipped a number of toggle switches to energize circuits for the main generators, the diesel engines, the signal lights, and the headlight. All four air gauge pointers were at the proper pressures. He flashed his dimly burning headlight at the "head man" (the brakeman on the head end of a train) who had walked down to the track switch which would allow them to enter the long running track connecting the outbound locomotive track with the freight yard.

With one of numerous explicit hand signals used in railroading, the head man motioned the hoghead to "come ahead" and then threw the switch into alignment for the running track. The hoghead moved the reverse lever into forward position, tolled the locomotive bell in case engine house workers were around, and pushed the independent (locomotive) air brake lever clockwise into release position, causing compressed air to hiss in the cab. Finally, he slowly advanced his throttle lever from "idle" to "1" and then "2" and "3"

(LR). The heavy units eased forward as their diesel engines began to chant ever louder in response to the electrical commands initiated by the throttle. He tested the air brakes briefly (TR 1001R) while rolling toward the switch to pick up his head man. The units shook the ground at 5 m.p.h. On the running track, the hoghead advanced the throttle to "6," increasing the diesels' roar, and briefly, their speed to 20 m.p.h. He quickly closed the throttle to "idle," waited ten seconds (LR), and pushed his dynamic brake lever into its braking position and then gently pushed it forward in order to test the electrical *dynamic* braking system, so vital for retarding his train on the downgrades ahead of him several hours from now. With a murmuring whine, the units responded to the electrical braking and almost came to a stop. The "dynamic" was in good order—at least for now. Back to the throttle and on to the freight yard where switch engines, like busy ants, would be moving cars to and fro.

The cars of the FCF awaited them on outbound track 20. The clearance form had a notation: "61{loads} - 19{empties} - 4263{tons}," not counting the four units. This was the make up of the FCF sitting in the just rising sun and consisting of conventional boxcars and long flatcars loaded with pairs of highway trailers carried "piggyback." Johnson backed against the cars, using his independent brakes. A dull clink of the heavy couplers indicated the units were mated to the FCF. Reflexively he had released most of his independent air braking pressure as he slowed to a stop, thereby preventing the locomotive wheels from sliding at slow speed under heavy air brake pressure. Next, the air hose was coupled by hand between the last unit and the first car. The hoghead pumped air with his diesel-driven compressors and charged the automatic air brake system running the length of his train. When he had the system charged, a number of car "toads" (car repairmen) began to inspect the brakes of the train (MR 1022, 1024, 1025A-H), after placing a blue flag on the 907 and on the caboose (OR 26). For their own safety the car toads used railroading's blue signal, which for English-speaking peoples is a highly re-

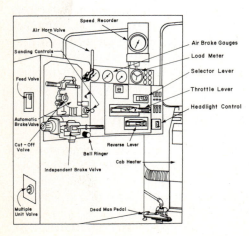

Controls in cab at engineer's workspace.

strictive symbol indicating stop/danger (Gamst 1975b:282–283, 292). After the "air test" of the brakes had been made, the head car toad gave lantern signal 8(g), "release air brakes," and the hoghead answered with engine whistle signal 14(b), "brakes released." Other occupants of the yard then began to respond to the two long whistle blasts of signal 14(b).

Yard engine 1312 which had been shunting cars on the running track of the outbound yard shoved its cars into the clear on track 15 and waited. "On spot [rest] at last" called the hoghead of the 1312 to his switchmen down on the ground. He poured himself the last of his night's coffee from a thermos as the other men on his crew walked down to the switchmen's shanty to hear the latest rail news and gossip.

Finishing its nightly round of servicing industries lying east of the terminal, the night local was pulling slowly off the main line—the throttle in "the over-time notch"—and creeping into outbound track 4, which a yard engine had earlier cleared of cars in order to receive the local. Old Ron Perkins was the local's hoghead; he was the number six man on the seniority list of several hundred. In his office, a converted wooden boxcar, the *yardmaster* drummed his fingers impatiently next to the buttons controlling the loudspeakers mounted throughout the yard. He decided not to use them as he stared over his desk out of the bay window in front of him. Better not to say anything or the old man would even go even slower. He could report Perkins' speed to one of the two *road foremen of engines,* the company officers who supervise locomotive engineers and firemen, but that would be pointless. Both road foremen had "fired" steam locomotives for Perkins decades ago and always showed some deference to him. They would mention to Perkins that the yardmaster (who, after all, was promoted from the ranks of the switchmen and not from those of the anointed, the enginemen) had complained; dismiss the complaint with a light word; and "old head it" (reminisce) with Perkins—"Remember Ronnie when I was firing the 2295 for you on that stormy night and we were low on water and couldn't get to the next plug without stabbing the varnish?" (We could not get to the next water tank without delaying a passenger train.)

Finally, the frustrated yardmaster yelled over his loudspeakers mounted near the FCF, "O.K. Clint, you can come on out now." At least Johnson was not temperamental as were some of these Goddamn hogheads who thought they owned the railroad, the yardmaster mused to himself. In the cab of the 907, Johnson smiled as the caboose of the night local left the running track, at 3 m.p.h. "You have to drive stakes to see if Ronnie is moving," he called down to a carman standing under the cab window.

The hoghead began moving his eighty cars one at a time as he stretched the several inches of slack in each coupler between the cars. After he had moved about sixty feet, the empty caboose began to roll. He picked up his head man and rolled his train down to the junction with the main line—governed by a *block signal*—which was . . .

"Red over green," called the head man from across the cab (OR 34, 240M).

"Red over green," the hoghead responded. "Here we go."

The conductor and rear brakeman were down on the ground "rolling the train by," that is, inspecting each car as it rolled past. The hoghead held his speed to 10 m.p.h. as he entered the main line at the block signal. He counted the telegraph poles along the main line so that he could gauge when the distant caboose would approach the two crew members on the ground to his rear. As the caboose passed them, the speed had been cut to 4 m.p.h. and the crew for the "rear end" of the train climbed aboard easily with their heavy grips in hand.

"Highball, Extra 907 East," came the cry over the train radio from the conductor on the caboose (OR 650–654). Interestingly, the hand signal and verbal command known as the "highball" (authority for a train to proceed) are not listed in any of the rules and regulations of the railroad.

"Highball," responded the hoghead after he depressed the broadcast button on his radio microphone. The company expected the hoghead to get the train over the road (BR 29), and that is what he would do.

When he entered the main line, Johnson moved his headlight control switch from "dim" to "front-full," thereby signaling with the cyclopian eye of the 907 that his train was occupying the main line (OR 17, 17A–17F, 18). Using the throttle, he slowly stretched the slack in his train. When the entire train was on the main line, he accelerated, slowly widening on the throttle to its final notch, "8" (LR). The roar of the four diesel engines behind him was deafening, all out of proportion to the low speed and slow acceleration being made. Sparks and gray smoke belched from the exhaust stacks in the roof of

Leaving town and accelerating with heavy exhaust on twenty-three-car No. 102, City of San Francisco.

each unit. To forestall wheel slippage and a possible train-breaking surge in the power being applied to the rails, the hoghead had turned on his front sanders which spewed dry sand onto the rail head to increase adhesion with his *drivers* (powered wheels)—six pairs per unit. With his throttle in the run "8" position he would burn 130 gallons of diesel fuel in ten minutes. The cost of fuel on an average trip exceeded his wages. The engines continued their tortured roar as the pointer on the speedometer slowly crept up the scale, 30, 40, then 50 m.p.h. As he approached 60 m.p.h., the hoghead began to "ease off" on his throttle. By now dust and bits of debris were swirling around beneath the train as it rushed over the heavy, well-maintained track, and a breeze blew through the open cab windows.

Consulting his eighty-page operating *timetable* (marked "For Employees Only"), the hoghead calculated that he could get to Morgan in time to take the siding for No. 9, the *Fast Flying Mail,* a scheduled first-class train *superior* to his *extra train* (not in the timetable). He had two cars to set out at Ridgeway some 100 miles away, but he did not think he could get there before 54, *The Overland Express,* overtook him from the west at 90 m.p.h. Rather than chance delaying the crack passenger train, he might have to head in at the Cementon passing track just to the west of Ridgeway and then follow 54 eastward for his switching. Meyers, the conservative conductor, would confer with the hoghead on that move. "What? Chance stabbing 54? Not while I'm in charge of this train," Meyers would storm. "And don't try and gain time by running at 75 [m.p.h.]," he would admonish. It would probably be Cementon then.

"Clear," he replied to the head man who had called the next signal, which was a single green. Moving along at 70 m.p.h., their speed for unrestricted track, a small white sign marked "W" rushed toward them on the right-hand side of the roadbed. The hoghead began to sound the standard highway crossing signal (OR 14L) on his whistle, actually an air horn. A red Volkswagen beetle moving at moderate speed approached the crossing, without slowing, at right angles to the train rushing over the countryside. Because the VW's windows were rolled up and the stereo radio was blaring at a high volume, the driver did not hear the air horn until the last second. However, he did eventually notice the flashing red warning lights at the railroad crossing—almost too late—and came to an abrupt halt before the highway crossing signals. Had the hoghead hit the auto, it would have taken almost two miles before he could bring the train to a stop on the very slight downgrade it had just entered. The massive steel snowplow *pilot* on the lower front of the 907 was a descendant of the wooden frame cow catcher of a century ago. It would have smashed and deflected the auto. With 740 tons of locomotive pulling 4200 tons of train at 70 m.p.h., the auto's passengers would have been crushed beyond recognition; they did not seem to realize this as the train thundered past. Peering up through their windshield they saw the engineer at his controls. The hoghead's stomach muscles relaxed. Having crossed over the highway, his mind was now on the ten cars they would pick up at Groveton Yard and the switching that this would entail. Out the window a yellow sign marked "65–55" flashed past him (OR 12D). The first number was the speed restriction for passenger trains and the second was for freights. He pulled his automatic brake valve lever into the application zone and first drew off 6 "pounds" of compressed air and then 4 more pounds from the *train line* running the length of the FCF, and charged to 90 pounds per square inch (MR 1005A, 1040). Compressed air roared into the cab as the train began to slow for the 55 m.p.h. (for freight trains) curve lying 2,500 feet ahead. Just beyond the curve would be block signal No. 37.2 which could be flashing yellow, if the day local had not yet cleared the main line. Better hold the reduction of train line pressure at 80 pounds per square inch (p.s.i.) until he could see the color of the signal. He still had most of his trip ahead of him.

The passengers in the Volkswagen had seen the engineer in his locomotive, a sight familiar to everyone in the United States and Canada. But they did not even begin to comprehend his activities in his rail world, one set apart from the everyday world by a number of circumstances which will be discussed in this book. The hoghead has an occupation which is highly visible in a very narrow sense; he is seen by all and extolled in legend. However, his work and his way of life are virtually unknown to nonrailroaders in our industrial urban society. This book will give the reader a still broader view of the rail world, just introduced by this section.

INDUSTRIAL ETHNOLOGY

As organized in North America, ethnology (social and cultural anthropology) is one of the four customary fields of anthropology, which also includes archeology, biological anthropology, and anthropological linguistics. Just as ethnologists may study industry, so too may anthropologists who are professionals in one of the other three fields of the discipline. Industrial archeology and industrial physical anthropology have been practiced for decades (Gamst 1975:37–39, 1977:2) and industrial linguistics in anthropology is also being developed (Tway 1977:24).

Ethnology is the comparative study of existing human cultures and societies, that is man's lifeways and social organizations. Ethnology often investigates behavior and groupings of a particular kind, for example, peasantries, hunters and gatherers, industrial groups, medical practices, religious organizations, and so forth. Ethnology uses data obtained by research in the field and from published and other sources, for example, documents in archives. The largely factually descriptive, but at least partially analytic, published volumes of ethnologists are called ethnographic monographs and include the book you are now reading. (The series, Case Studies in Cultural Anthropology—edited by George and Louise Spindler—contains a wide range of representative ethnographic monographs. See the back cover of this monograph.) Such monographs ordinarily result from a particular long-term field study by an ethnologist, such as my own concerning railroaders or the Qemant peasantry of Ethiopia (Gamst 1969).

More and more ethnologists are adding the study of industrial urban societies to their traditional study of tribal and agrarian societies (see Gamst 1974:3–18). As yet, relatively few ethnologists (see Gamst 1977) have turned their attention to the industrial (or work) sectors of modern urban civilization (for example, Pilcher 1972). Industrial ethnology is based upon a significant change in the setting of customary ethnological fieldwork but not necessarily in theory or in research techniques and methodology.

The ethnological study of industry comprises a significant part of the ethnological study of work—of all occupations—industrial and nonindustrial, Western and non-Western. The scope of this book is limited to a major industry of the United States and Canada, railroading, but the method and theory involved have wider applicability in North America and elsewhere. The subject of research in this book, like most of the ethnological study of industry in North America, cannot be considered trivial or exotic, but is a study of middle America.

In accord with definitions found in dictionaries, used by industrial sociologists and psychologists, and employed by Federal agencies such as the Bureau of Labor Statistics, an *industry* is a distinctive branch of productive work on a large scale, including its capital and labor. As a concept, an industry represents an analytic grouping of business *firms* such as factories, stores, government agencies, mines, and transportation companies producing goods and/or services. In labeling certain societies, such as the United States and Canada, with the term "industrial," social scientists call attention to fundamental societal characteristics. With regard to these characteristics, the industrial sociologist Eugene Schneider says that we "imply that in innumerable direct and indirect ways industrialism places its stamp on our culture as a whole; that it shapes men's lives, molds our institutions, and in the long run helps shape the values, ideals, and goals of society as a whole" (1969:1).

Generally speaking, with regard to occupational social organizations, industrial ethnology investigates subcultures of industrial work. Investigation covers behavioral and attitudinal patterns of workers, symbols important to workers, paths of communication within work organizations, places of work and their physical arrangements, and social interaction of workers with co-workers and others both on and off the job. Investigation also includes study of the absence of work among certain people, for example, the unemployed and the retired. Following holistic inclinations in anthropology, industrial ethnology is more than just the study of occupational organizations and their institutions; it is also the investigation of relations among such organizations and of their relations with the wider societal order. Investigation of the various kinds just mentioned has ends both basic and practical for the understanding of industry, work, and occupation.

The Dictionary of Occupational Titles published by the Department of Labor defines 22,000 job titles, thereby reflecting the overwhelming diversity of the division of labor in the United States. The highly complex division of labor into multitudinous specializations within industrial society makes it impossible to study in depth all of an ethnic group (that is, a specific culture) such as the Yankees or the Anglo-Canadians. However, this division is associated with numerous occupational subcultures, which frequently provide a ready-made unit of study. Especially well bounded socially are industries such as coal mining, stevedoring, railroading, trucking, inland and oceanic shipping, logging, farming, fishing, law enforcement, the military, and certain kinds of manufacturing.

Not all industrial groups amenable to ethnological inquiry need to be large or well bounded. Those whose sociological endeavor is grounded in the participant observation of work, remark: "Any social group, to the extent that it is a distinctive unit, will have to some degree a culture differing from that of other groups, a somewhat different set of common understandings around which action is organized" (Becker and Geer 1957:29).

Industrial study in ethnology is distinguishable from the study of industry in other disciplines in a number of ways. Foremost among these is the use of "a set of assumptions about 'culture' as a master concept in terms of which human behavior is broadly explainable" (Pelto 1970:18 and cf. also Gamst and Norbeck 1976). The concept of holistic culture provides a generalized theory common to almost all ethnologists and most other anthropologists in the other fields of the discipline. This theory is in part an implicit frame of reference for ordering the sociocultural realm (Pelto 1970:17–20,64). "Holism" sometimes refers to the study of a group in its entirety, but it more properly refers broadly to the all-inclusive nature of the base concepts worked with by ethnologists (culture, society, modal personality, geographic environment). In accordance with these concepts, ethnology attends to matters of context of a social act or network of acts in ways customarily more thorough than those of the other, more singular, social sciences.

Related to the holistic cultural theory are implicit assumptions used in method regardless of whether or not explicit methods of the same kind are directly used. A basic methodology entails use of a cross-cultural perspective, even when studying our own native subcultures. The underlying cross-cultural perspective channels and limits what ethnologists say about our own occupational subcultures.

Cultural data used by ethnologists are "emic" at least to some degree; that is, an emic methodology is invariably applied in collection and analysis of data. By "emic" is meant a broad method where data are gathered and organized from the insider's or native's viewpoint and logic of classification, rather than from an outsider's and alien classification made in advance of a research project. An emic approach has been a tenet of ethnology since the fieldwork of pioneers such as Franz Boas and Bronislaw Malinowski in the early decades of this century. Outside of ethnology, research into new areas of inquiry usually involves gathering and organizing sociocultural data according to the canons of scientific hypothesis testing, but at the same time according to what might be considered an *a priori* bias, that is, according to a hypothesis accounting for some part of sociocultural reality before it is at all known. At times, the hypothesis in whole or in part becomes what could be called a "self-fulfilling hypothesis," as data are unwittingly selected or tailored to illustrate the theory. Ethnology's emic methodology helps guard against the danger of self-fulfilling hypothesis, or what Francis Bacon called a "pernicious predetermination" in which "the first conclusion colors and brings into conformity with itself all that comes after, though far sounder and better" (Bacon [1620]:50–51). The important distinction is that for the ethnologist the hypothesis usually emerges as the fieldwork progresses and it is not preformulated. Both the hypothesis and the specifics of methodology are emergent: They develop from the experience of the ethnologist in the field of social action being studied.

Ethnology's central mode of operation is formed by joining the underlying cultural theory and methodologies with its basic, but not sole, technique of research—participant observation. To this central mode, various explicit theories and techniques may be added as needed, for example, aspects of role theory and survey research. The basic technique gives ethnologists a first-hand contact with their subject matter and subjects, which is not the norm in other social sciences. An ethnology of modern industry attempts to narrow the ever-widening gap between conceptualization concerning work and the sociocultural elements and settings of work.

In the ethnological view, the extent to which social scientists can understand human behavior has a limitation when such understanding is methodologically based largely upon *periodic* investigation—in survey research, in observation without meaningful participation, and in formal interviewing—instead of based upon the *continuous* participant observation central to ethnological method. Ethnologists have long known that such a limitation exists in the study of tribal, peasant, and preindustrial urban peoples. Similarly, it is present in any study of the multitudinous occupational organizations of the industrial urban world. Here, most occupations are all but unknown to the average person, including the typical social scientist about to study one of the occupations. A prime example is the occupation of locomotive engineer. Industrial ethnology overcomes the methodological limitation to understanding behavior in industry through its customary style of research, which is normally conducted not only continuously but in great depth, including investigation of patterning of culture on the ideal, believed, and actual/behavioral levels. Studies conducted by other social scientists concerned with man in an industrial setting usually have much shallower foci (invariably statistical) than do those conducted by ethnologists. A major exception is certain industrial sociological studies based upon participant observation, which sociologists usually term "anthropological" method. The nonethnological foci usually result in the depiction of a largely ideal culture. Ideal cultural patterns include verbalized ones that are "oughts" and "shoulds" rather than actually observable.

Ethnological study is normally one of great flexibility because its primary qualitative focus in method can produce more new ideas and empirical data than do more rigidly conceived and organized methods of other social sciences. This is especially so where the latter are primarily oriented to quantitative research, with emphasis on sampling and statistical techniques and on survey research and quantified archival data. Ethnology can give contextual significance and validation to quantitative research, which can, and should, be made a valuable adjunct to industrial ethnological method. Of course, a degree of quantification is needed in all ethnology. Certainly, a largely impressionistic ethnology of work will not suffice. Pragmatic and educated workingmen will not accept unverifiable artistic conjecture on their alleged "Apollonian" or "Dionysian" integrations of culture. Instead, they want an empirically based commentary on their social relations and ideological patterning. Most likely, one can get by with far less in writing about coal miners than in writing about an ethnography concerning a now defunct tribe as seen through the eyes of one fieldworker.

In industrial society, the specific role used as a person's mark of rank and general identification of the self is usually his occupational role. "What do you do?" we ask as our first meaningful question after the ritual form "How do you do?" In the United States and Canada, we often talk about the decline of the work ethic, the worker's disinterest in his work world, and the great development of leisure activities and interests. Despite all of this, the primary social identification of most Americans and Canadians is what they do, that is, their job. In industrial society the person who has lost his job is severely demoralized, and even more severe is the plight of the person who has not only lost his job, but additionally, has little hope of any comparable employment. The unemployed feel ostracized at social gatherings, and rightly so. They often stand in a corner having little to discuss with others since conversations frequently center or at least touch upon the world of work. Usually, with no job, one has little public identity or publicly presentable image of the self.

In industrial society, work and occupational role constitute the focal point of a person's life. (Of course access to an occupational role is often contingent upon various ascriptive factors relating to a person's overall status including race, ethnicity, sex, age, and statuses of parents.) We spend as many as twenty-one years in formal educational preparation for our work during the first part of our life, for example, to reach the level of the doctorate. In the middle, and largest, part of our life span we devote half of our waking hours to our occupation each work day and often several more hours in commuting to and from work. Furthermore, work is used to accumulate wealth so that we may retire, frequently to a workless oblivion, during the final part of our life span. Occupational role determines to a large extent one's standard of living, including the quality and variety of one's food, clothing, and other possessions; the size and location of one's domicile(s); the kind of people with whom one associates; and the quality of educational, medical, and legal services; in short, one's entire social and psychic well-being.

"Without work all life goes rotten. But when work is soulless, life stifles and dies."—Albert Camus

"Blessed be he who has found his work; let him ask no other blessedness."—Thomas Carlyle

"You take my life if you take the means whereby I live."—William Shakespeare

2/The railroad and its setting

In this chapter we will examine some of the historic backgrounds of railroading in general and those of the CC & U in particular. We will consider the technologic and economic place of railroads in American society and the importance of studying the geographic setting of a railroad such as the CC & U.

Ethnologists have always been interested in the historic antecedents of the institutions they investigate in order to provide a long-term reliable context for their data and ideas. Cultural patterns are not temporally isolated; they originate in the past, continue through the present, and develop into the future. Their present state results from what they were; and what they are conditions what they will be (Hoebel 1972:15). Ethnology has always included an interest in the "life histories" of groups, "irrespective of their degree of advancement" (Kroeber 1948:5). This applies to Masai herdsmen as well as to Portland longshoremen. The historic element in ethnology supplements the functionalist element (Radcliffe-Brown 1935). Further, ethnologists ordinarily report on the geographic setting of their investigations in providing an understanding of the ecological basis of the group studied (Gamst and Norbeck 1976:247–249; Radcliffe-Brown 1952). As technology evolves and increases in its capacity to use energy and multiply human effort, geography has a proportionately lesser control upon man's lifeways. However, even in technologic eras of machines powered by the steam engine and then by the internal combustion engine, geography restricts human activity, as we shall see in the case of the CC & U.

DEVELOPMENT OF RAILROADS AND THE UNITED STATES

When the average person thinks of railroading, he often reflects upon its colorful history—upon the winning of the West and upon cowboys and Indians and railroaders. Far more than most of us realize, the railroads have been fundamental in the industrialization, economic development, and social transformation of the agrarian United States after the era of Presidents Jefferson and Jackson. Railroads are one of the oldest industries of the industrial/fossil fuel revolution, both in Great Britain and in the United States. Without railroads the societal transformation of Europe and North America by an industrial revolution could not have taken place. The earliest railroads were not common carriers as most are today. (Common carriers are transportation firms regulated by government and operating under a franchise, or special right to conduct business in a territory conferred by government, and engaged in transport of freight or passengers for a price governed by regulated rates.) Early railroads hauled minerals, usually coal and stone, for a private firm from the quarry or mine to waterborne shipping. Single or coupled freight carts were propelled along wooden rails by horse and ox power on level track and upgrades, and by gravity on the downgrades.

One of the first railroads in the United States, patterned upon a century of earlier development of colliery railroads in Great Britain, was the Quincy Granite Railroad of the Boston area. Beginning in 1826 the railroad used oxen and gravity to haul carloads of granite from the Blue Hills south of Boston to tidewater barges at a pier on the Neponset River of Boston. (Some of the stone was used by Daniel Webster and others to construct the Bunker Hill Monument, an obelisk overlooking Boston Harbor.) After starting out as a canal company, the oldest common carrier railroad is still in operation as the Delaware and Hudson Railroad. In 1823 the Delaware and Hudson Canal Company began hauling coal on rails in Pennsylvania by means of gravity and a then new British railroad innovation—a stationary steam engine, located inside an engine house, which used a rope to pull cars upgrade. The next step was to replace the draft animals on level track by making the housed steam engine a locomotive vehicle. By 1825, early British and American mechanical engineers had the steam engine successfully pumping a pair of driving wheels on a railcar. The car was consequently self-propelled, or locomotive. (The word "locomotive" was an adjective before it was a noun.) The canals, and the railroad draft animals, were doomed; the industrial revolution had been given the high-capacity, reliable land transportation needed for its triumph over the older agrarian technology and social order which had spawned it.

It could be said that the "rail roads," as they were then known, made a transition of energy conversion around 1830. In the transition, the steam engine, both stationary and locomotive, replaced the two earlier forms of power, draft animals and gravity. (Railroads made another such transition in the mid-twentieth century when the more efficient internal combustion diesel replaced the external combustion steam engine.) By the 1830s the steam engine, with its "engineman," had become more efficient than the draft animal, which needed a "carter" to control movement of the car, and more efficient than the limited applications of gravity, which needed a "brakeman" alone to hand brake the car downhill against the pull of the grade. When I say "more efficient," I refer to the difference between energy input and output of a vehicle system and, consequently, to its ability as an energy converting system to multiply human effort. It should be noted here that the craft of brakeman predates that of railway engineman by a century or more. Before the advent of the air brake, enginemen whistled their brakemen to "tie down" hand brakes to retard the momentum of their train of many cars.

At the beginning of the industrial/fossil fuel revolution, even the most primitive of coal mines had a miner producing about 1000 times as much energy in coal as he expended in producing it. Such a miner multiplied his human muscle power through hand tools and rail carts pushed through the mine by hand. (Since the Middle Ages, Europeans used carts pushed on wooden rails in and around mines. This technology is the origin of all railroading.) With increased mechanical mining processes multiplying the human effort in excavating coal, the rate of energy return in the collieries became staggering, even at deeper flood-prone levels. Energy converters such as steam sump pumps, steam mine hoists, and stationary and locomotive steam engines for hauling cars around the mine area and over long distances to market all added to the free or surplus energy contributed to the industrializing economies of Western Europe and North America (cf. Cottrell 1964:707–708, 1970:11–13). These additions of free energy gave Euro-America an economic, and hence political, advantage over the rest of the world that has not been lost to this day.

Common carrier railroads added still more free energy to the Euro-American economies in energy/labor savings on cartage of goods, passengers, and communications—especially mail. Railroads cut the time of delivery for all three, besides creating demands and markets not previously possible because of high cost of transport. Accelerated rail shipment of goods also released capital that had formerly been tied up in materials enroute between seller and purchaser. This capital was freed as profit, which was used in part for investment fostering further economic development. Railroads conquered distance as a barrier to economic development.

Even today in areas of the world where railways or modern highways are scarce, time and distance have not been reduced in commerce and, consequently, these areas are little developed, and prosperity is on a very low level. Both historically and presently, regions with little or no modern transport are so vast to their inhabitants, that most such people live and die in their native and neighboring villages, never having traveled more than a few days' walk from their homes. The region of the Qemant peasantry of Ethiopia (Gamst 1969) illustrates this point. It is certainly easy to see why in the nineteenth century the railroads and their locomotives were symbols and metaphors of progress and development. In *Walden*, published in 1854, Henry David Thoreau gives us a vivid example:

> [W]hen I hear the iron horse make the hills echo with his snort like thunder, shaking the earth with his feet, and breathing fire and smoke from his nostrils (what kind of winged horse or fiery dragon they will put into the new mythology I don't know), it seems as if the earth has got a race worthy to inhabit it.

Besides facilitating the low-priced mass transport of raw materials and manufactured goods, and the cheap reliable movement of people, railroads were one of the earliest of the industrial big businesses, providing many models of organization and procedure for other industry. Railroad managers were therefore necessarily pioneers in industrial finance, labor relations, industrial safety, relations with government and its regulations, and in problems of competition from within and without a particular industry. The size, complexity, and importance of railroads determined that their managers had to grapple with and set patterns for industrial organization before other industrial managers were compelled to do so. Also, by creating a massive demand for iron, steel, coal, and capital goods, such as locomotives and cars and accessories of these, the railroads along with the cotton goods industry helped usher in the industrial revolution. Large-scale and continuous railroad consumption of products of mill and mine created a demand for all manner of supportive financial, manufacturing, mining, commercial, and engineering activity. This activity was exceedingly important in allowing Great Britain and, somewhat later, the United States to achieve the earliest of the world's self-sustained economic modernizations. In these two countries snowballing techno-economic development had reached, by the mid-nineteenth century, the "take off" point, a point not yet reached by most of the countries of today's world, which are consequently known as developing states.

The railroads did not just furnish transportation for the first industrial development out of the age-old, agrarian, socioeconomic order, in large part they underwrote the cost of that development. For example, without the production of enormous amounts of iron and steel for the railroad lines and equipment, the price of steel would not have declined sufficiently and the technology for working steel would not have developed sufficiently to stimulate the evolution in the late nineteenth century of other industries upon a base of inexpensive and plentiful steel.

The railroad boom of the 1840s necessitated the raising of awesomely large amounts of money, for the first time in the history of capitalism. No longer could banks in the area of a railroad and local interested citizenry provide the funds needed to underwrite construction and equipping of a railroad. Money markets across Europe and North America had to be tapped. Capitalists were thereby transformed into truly impersonal (faceless) investors of funds for return at a profit in an often far-off and little-known place. Thus the technologic and economic scale and organization of the railroad industry forced a fundamental development of capitalism into a more efficient, fluid state of raising investment funds. The New York stock and bond exchanges developed with the growth of American railroads.

As pioneers of industry, railroad managers blazed a trail to be followed by others. Thus they were the first to communicate managerial information on a large scale to one another—through organizing industry-wide and regional committees, holding industrial conferences, and publishing business journals such as the *Railway Gazette*. Because of the early development of strong labor unions in the railroad operating crafts (1870 to 1900), the influence and constraint of organized labor upon management occurred in the railroads long before it did in other industries. Owing in part to the complexity of the various aspects of railroading (operations, building and servicing rolling stock, and constructing and maintaining right of way and structures), managers tended to work all of their lives in railroading as they acquired the necessary experience for efficient management. These expert old managers gradually wrested control of the carriers from their owners, the stockholders. The managers allocated revenue in part for current operations, in part for future betterments and expansion, and in part for the dividends on investment to the stockholders. The owners had to be contended with periodically as at their annual meetings, but not continuously. So began the first of the transfers of control of an industrial firm from the owners to the managers.

By 1900 a network of steel rails was interlaced across the continent of North America, which was highly industrialized in its Canadian and United States regions. The era of railroad building was essentially completed. One of the capstones to this era of construction was the CC & U. The period of American railroad building and the specific contributions of railroads to American development between 1840 and 1900 is well documented in specialized and general studies and thus will not be treated further here. (For a contradictory view of the importance of the railroad in American development see Fogel 1964.)

Because of its widespread network, the railroad industry, in contrast to most other heavy industries, exists in almost every county of the contiguous United States. Its terminal centers, in which railroaders reside and many work, are found like well-spaced beads along the trunk lines. Railroads are thus an omnipresent industry in this country. Some parts of the country are too thickly covered by railroads for the amount of available business. About two-thirds of the rail freight transported by the country's 58 major common carrier railroads is concentrated on one-fifth of our 193,500 mile rail system. One-third of the network, 60,000 miles, produces only one percent of the traffic.

RAILROADS IN CONTEMPORARY AMERICAN SOCIETY

Today, the highly integrated economic system of the United States would come to a halt with a stoppage of rail freight service. Most industries have just a few day's supply of parts needed for production. Railroads are extensions of assembly lines and can be considered extended conveyor belts of components from the plants that make them to those that assemble them; for example the Michigan auto part fabricators linked by numerous railroads to the regional auto assembly plants. Along the CC & U, Farmer Brown is a large meat packing firm in Urbana and dependent upon five Pork Livestock (PLS) trains per week for its porcine output. The PLS rushes across the hot steppe at night, climbs the final mountain range at near-passenger train speed, and arrives at Urbana Yard between 4:00 and 5:00 A.M., in time for the necessary 6:00 A.M. spotting of the slatted cars of hogs at the Farmer's spur. No slow freights get in the way of the fast, stench-ridden PLS. A yard engine is always standing by to receive the stock cars. Freight cars of all kinds also function as

Railroaders on strike for a few days. The federal government does not allow national rail strikes to endure for more than one or two days because of the necessity of rail freight for the country's well-being.

both stationary and movable storage containers. Enroute, they are rolling inventories, sometimes changing ownerships and destination before reaching a final terminal. When at the terminal, they may sit idle for days at low rental to the shipper, serving as mini-warehouses for products of mine, mill, and forest. Railroads inefficiently rent new $32,000 freight cars for a few dollars a day to customers who cannot, or will not, unload their freight.

The vital rail distribution system of the United States (which is interrelated with those of Canada and Mexico) is complex and highly coordinated. Consequently, skilled, responsible managers and operating personnel are needed to make it function properly and efficiently. Loaded cars and unneeded empties must be brought in from plants and warehouses and new empties and loads must be given to them as needed. The outbound loads must be switched into *blocks* of cars by yard crews under supervision of a yardmaster for inclusion in trains, and these are then inspected, serviced, and sometimes repaired by carmen under supervision of a car foreman.

A suitable locomotive for the train must be assembled from available units and serviced and tested at the engine house under supervision of a roundhouse foreman. A crew dispatcher calls the proper, rested road crew. The train leaves the jurisdiction of the yardmaster and is guided by the train dispatcher over a road crowded with other through freight, local switching freight, and passenger movements. Outbound trains are given loads and empties to set out enroute at designated sites. Long *blocks* of cars are routed to appropriate terminals, perhaps thousands of miles from the yard in which they were first switched together. At a distant terminal another yardmaster receives the train, and his switch crews distribute its cars to customers of the railroad and to other railroads.

THE GEOGRAPHICAL SETTING OF THE CC & U

Geography places limits upon rail transportation which even the most modern and energy-intensive technology cannot entirely overcome. Two such limiting factors are topography and, to a lesser extent, weather. Trains are sensitive to grades. A CC & U freight with four 1750 h.p. diesel units pulling a 3400-ton train can make 50 to 60 m.p.h. most of the way from Urbana Yard to Piedmont, but will grind up the grade of 2.2 percent out of Piedmont over the Maxwell Pass at 8 to 10 m.p.h. This performance will be repeated further east on the CC & U over similar mountain grades. (In comparison, modern interstate highways usually have a maximum grade of 5 percent and older roads may have gradients twice as steep.) Certain light, high-speed freight trains with large amounts of motive power, for instance around 15,000 h.p., can negotiate the 2.2 percent grade at 25 or even 40 m.p.h., the latter being a passenger train speed for this particular area.

The CC & U has three long grades of 2 percent or more, two of about 1.5 percent, and many lesser grades of about 1 percent. According to CC & U hogheads, even these lesser grades are a challenge, and would be even more of a challenge to crews on the (derisively termed) "pool table railroads" of certain regions of North America. "When you take a 10,000 ton coal or ore train over our property, you know how to railroad," challenged hoghead McLeod to a visiting "rail" (operating railroader) from the Midwest. Generally, the grades on the CC & U are steeper running from west to east. In fact, it is on these eastbound runs that diesel units often experience mechanical or electrical failure, especially on a hot summer day while in the teeth of the grade.

A geological explanation exists for the series of severe grades on the eastbound CC & U and many other western lines. Most of the earth's surface is divided into a number of crustal plates, for example, an African plate, a North American plate, and a Pacific plate. The plates move as rigid structures over the hotter, semiplastic, underlying level of the earth. The collision of the vast Pacific and North American plates results in the plates buckling and causes earth tremors. Mountain ranges rise when the earth buckles, in this case forming steeper slopes toward the west or Pacific plate, which is being slowly pushed under the North American plate. (Therefore, it is not true, as prophets of doom predict, that parts of California will fall into the Pacific Ocean. Actually, parts of California will eventually disappear under Nevada and Arizona.) The ranges are made of crustal material folded upward and downward under the plate's slow compressive motion of a few centimeters per year. Thus a geological process covering many tens of millions of years fosters a topographic profile which affects the work of operating railroaders and occasionally leads to a burnt out locomotive unit on the upgrade or a runaway train on the downgrade.

Mountains and hilly terrain often involve sharp curves which must be negotiated at low speeds. Many of the tight curves on railroads were constructed using nineteenth century technology, which was employed for most American gradients and alignments before the end of the era of railroad building, around 1910. Much of American rail roadbeds was constructed with explosives, hand labor, and draft animals—for example, a mule team and a scraper-board grader used to move and level earth. Gradually, the railroads are reducing gradients, easing tight curves, and increasing the bore of tunnels. However, much of the original restriction on railroad topographic profiles still exists. Thus at the top of Maxwell Pass on the mountainous rise out of Piedmont, a number of 20 and 30 m.p.h. curves, which were created by machines from before the internal combustion era, were eliminated only a few years ago by modern construction equipment. Further east down the line, a tight, old, timber-lined tunnel was enlarged by "daylighting" it, that is, by removing with diesel cranes and tractors approximately 200 feet of overburden including over 300,000 cubic yards of stone. This would have been a near-impossible feat when the line was built around the turn of the century.

The region traversed by the CC & U can be described in one climatological word—arid. It is part of the northern region of the two broad belts of desert and semidesert (steppe) which cover the land surface of the earth about 30° north and 30° south latitude. These dry belts are caused by circulation of the atmosphere, especially winds and high pressure zones associated with the seasonally prevailing cyclonic westerlies. The CC & U line crosses approximately 1000 miles of steppe and desert with some short, slightly verdant stretches. In the desert, it rains only a few inches, unevenly distributed throughout the year. In some areas this moisture supports various species of desert vegetation and small animals, but much of the ground is bare. Annuals, often with bright flowers, grow briefly at the end of any winter rain. The steppe areas, with up to ten inches of rain per year, have more grass, some scrub trees, and large animals such as deer. Larger trees line many of the washes. Some of the rain of the CC & U region is regular winter rain, moderate to almost nonexistent according to the area, generated by what is known as a Mediterranean climatic pattern. In this pattern, cyclonic westerly wind belts migrate to more southerly latitudes during the winter months, blowing westward onto the North American continent from the Pacific Ocean. The Mediterranean pattern gives the railroaders of the CC & U predictable rain, usually in moderate amounts, but sometimes in torrents which wash out the tracks. Snow also falls. Precipitation is heavier on the western slopes of mountains, and the descending westerly winds then dry the eastern slopes of the ranges. Nearer to the Pacific, the Mediterranean pattern generates periodic dense fog, which at times even climbs up over the mountains at Maxwell Pass.

During this recurrent dense fog, as long as wayside *block signals* are green, passenger trains hurtle along the track at 79 or 90 m.p.h. and freights at 50, 60, or 70 m.p.h., all traveling at the authorized maximum speed for each kind of train. As the white posts marked "W" (whistle) flash by, the hoghead sounds the standard crossing signal on his air horns, continuing it until the crossing is passed. The headlight, on full bright, makes an enormous yellow-white beacon at the head of the train, the beam reflecting off the dense fog and obscuring forward vision for more than a few feet. As soon as a somewhat restrictive signal flashes by the cab window from out of the foggy curtain, speed is reduced until the next signal comes into view. Should this one be still more restrictive, speed is greatly reduced, to 15 or 20 m.p.h., and may be reduced still more as the landmarks hearalding the next signal are passed. The next signal may suddenly be green and the crew in the cab will exchange their sighting of its aspect: "Clear." "Clear." (The green aspect is not called by its color-name, perhaps a survival from the time when the proceed signal had a clear "white" glass lens [Gamst 1975b:281–282,292].) Further down the track, the reason for the earlier, restrictive block signals appears in the mist. A local freight was gathering its cars and now, like a mother hen with her chicks, is safely in the clear on a passing track parallel to the main line.

The steppe and desert area also receive occasional summer rain generated by southwesterly monsoon and southeasterly anticyclonic winds which penetrate the continent from time to time. Both winter and summer storms at times drop several inches of water in a few hours, usually with severe consequences. Although well-cut canyons exist along parts of the CC & U's route, much of it is drained by periodic streams lacking well-defined beds, especially on the flats into which they flow. Flash flooding can occur in canyons and across level areas of the route. Flash floods rip out massive steel bridges and wash away long sections of track and its supporting roadbed. Destroyed track causes the block signal system to display red on either side of the damage. However, track, roadbed, and structures (such as bridges) that are rendered unstable but still in place represent a grave hazard, since they usually give no signal indication of their condition.

The CC & U suffered a devastating series of washouts of the roadbed in the first decade of its operation. Each year for three years a severe flood attacked the line. The last one was a rampaging Mediterranean cyclonic westerly, which caused flooding in several states and destroyed the track, roadbed, and many steel bridges around Crofts and in Long Canyon between Jackson and Topaz. Limited by turn-of-the-century technology, the reconstruction took six weeks, and many shippers along the line suffered. After the devastation, almost a million dollars was invested in buttressing the line through Long Canyon to insure rail service during severe storms in the future.

Three years passed without much problem until the appearance of a huge cyclonic westerly. Train No. 2, *The Transcon Flyer*—the pride and joy of the old CC & U ("DO NOT DELAY THIS TRAIN." P.M. Nelson, Superintendent)—made its regular ten-minute stop and crew change at Jackson on the January night of the storm and did not reach Central City until six months later. Long Canyon was hit the hardest of any section of the line as the floodwaters crested several feet above the expensive repair work and track relocations. In all, about 100 miles of line were totally destroyed between Reed and Crestview.

The following year, *The Transcon* was marooned for over one week in the once again flooded canyon. The next year, following two years of construction, a new line higher up the canyon wall was opened. Toward the end of the 1930s parts of the new, high line were washed out for three weeks, as was part of the line east of Crofts. In recent years flooding from both winter and summer storms still causes line washouts, but only in short sections. This is because modern construction technology, with its huge and powerful earth-moving machinery, has been better able to protect the line with rock ("rip-rap") buttressing, run-off channels, and earthen protective dams. When the line is breached, it is repaired in a day with a temporary track ("shoofly") running around the damage until the permanent way is restored, usually in a week or so.

Two division officers were fired not too long ago when a washout west of Orwell on Zenith Hill temporarily knocked out the block signals. The officers, Carstairs and Reynolds, were at the site dispatching trains up and down the mountain without the proper, restrictive, fail-safe protection of the operating rules. For this oversight, they were precipitously "dehorned" (fired from an officer's position) by system management. Operating railroaders often delight in recounting the story of a dehorning. The pattern of the story is

Union Pacific No. 104, City of Los Angeles, meets UP Extra 3608 West, stopped in Montclair siding against a red absolute "A" signal. A massive drainage ditch for flood protection is under construction between highway and railroad. Head man "highballs the varnish" (see glossary).

about the same each time. The general manager of the CC & U comes into town on his observation-platformed business car and orders Mr. Jones, a trainmaster, to meet his car at Jackson Depot at a certain time. The "G.M." tells Jones, "Your service as a trainmaster is no longer required. Exercise your seniority as trainman effective June 13." The firing and demotion of Jones to an ordinary brakeman is publicly announced in the bulletin books and proclaimed in the next numbered revision of the division employee's timetable where the entry, "J.R. JONES, trainmaster . . . Jackson" is replaced by, "N.B. LAWRENCE, trainmaster . . . Jackson." (All railroad officials, great and small, relate to others in the rail and the outside worlds from behind a pair of initials.)

Before leaving the subject of geographical controls on railroading, the elements of heat and wind should be mentioned. The steppe and desert are hot, sometimes oppressively so at over 110° F, in summer and early fall. Perishable freight can indeed spoil if train schedules are not maintained and special instructions are not followed—seeing that produce is properly cooled, and livestock is hosed down with water when necessary. Diesel units break down from the heat. The normal temperatures developed in the engine rooms are exceedingly hot, hot enough to pain a man's face as he goes about his rounds of troubleshooting on the units. Locomotive cabs are not air-conditioned, despite the enormous amounts of electrical power generated by a unit which could be used for this purpose. Needless to say, switching cars at a desert station during mid-day in the summer can be very enervating to a crew. Almost every year there are a few motorists who have an automobile break-down on the secondary roads of the great desert and die from the heat. CC & U crews have been instrumental in saving some of these desert wayfarers, but not always.

A recent newspaper account gives a typical example of death in the summer heat. A young Urbana couple vainly attempted to walk to safety when their camper truck was bogged down in loose sand only one-and-a-half miles from a CC & U station, where water facilities support some shade trees. They may have been disoriented in the intense, furnace-like heat and thus did not discern the direction of the trains passing nearby:

> Wednesday evening, a [CC & U] work crew found the abandoned camper truck and discovered [the man's] body about 4.5 miles away, where he apparently had fallen down an embankment.
>
> The body of [his wife] was found a half mile farther along. . . . Beside her was an empty water container.

Wind occasionally piles sand upon the tracks, even in the few verdant areas outside of the steppe and desert. Train orders warning of the possible dangerous covering of the tracks are then issued by the dispatcher. At times the wind acts as a sand blaster, turning windows opaque, removing paint from the equipment, rendering inoperative some of the electrical components of a locomotive, and sometimes disabling a unit altogether. Strong quartering winds, blowing against either forward corner of a train of freight cars, can increase train drag and slow down or even overload a locomotive.

3/Hiring out

Ethnologists are interested in how people are selected for and enculturated (socialized) in their roles, occupational or otherwise, in society. As new members are added to a group, in what ways are rewards and sanctions used to replicate the behavior of the present generation of role incumbents? Of course, old patterns are not entirely repeated and new patterns are continually added to meet changing circumstances (cf. Harris 1971:136–141). To shed light on these matters, we examine in this chapter the recruitment and early training and enculturation of engine service employees. Through the experiences of a "student," as novices are called, we learn about entry into the craft of engine service. We also become further acquainted with the rail world and with the job of the locomotive engineer. First, however, let us consider in a general way the craft and the training for it.

ENCULTURATING THE RAILROADER

Enculturation is the life-long process by which a person in a particular subculture of a culture (Gamst and Norbeck 1976:3–4) adapts to, and learns through instruction, imitation and habituation, and deduction, his changing social position and its appropriate roles—expected behaviors and attitudes (Gamst and Norbeck 1976:148–153,165–166). An example of a culture would be that of the Anglo–Americans, Zulu, Navajo, or Japanese. A subculture is a part of a whole culture, for example, that of railroaders among Anglo–Americans. During the enculturation process for his craft the "student" adjusts to the discipline and rhythm of the railroad and of the machine, especially the locomotive. Railroading is a twenty-four-hour-a-day, seven-day-a-week operation, standing in opposition to the prevailing temporal and social organization of American society. The locomotive is demanding in its precise requirements and unforgiving to those not heeding certain fundamental rules. Derailing or breaking a freight train into two or more segments of cars is an easy accomplishment for the negligent. However, some mechanical latitude exists for personal styles of train handling.

In the assembly lines and other mechanized productive processes of today, workers are usually dwarfed into insignificance, reduced to mere cogs, in the vast stream of production. Work is increasingly divided into a large number of very narrow and routine tasks requiring simple skills, and monotony is the hallmark of the mechanized occupation. Where the tasks are not just mechanized but truly automated, the worker is reduced to an often-bored observer of a part of the flow of production. This is not so with the locomotive engineer, who totally controls a locomotive and its train. Electrical power for operations does not come from a distant source not under his own control (for example, New York's Con Edison), but is generated according to his commands in his own personal powerhouse on rails. He not only generates electricity; he compresses air; causes fuel, lubricating oil, and water to be pumped; applies sand to the rails as needed; acts as a radio operator; converts electric motors to generators and generators to motors for various purposes; and is even concerned with the operation of a steam boiler (on many passenger units) used for heating passenger cars.

The engineer is not an extension of the machine; rather, the machine is an extension of his skills. The locomotive and train respond, and sometimes react adversely, to his manipulations and idiosyncracies. Certain appurtenances limit his absolute control; for example, cab signals, deadman surveillance devices, and penalty applications of the automatic braking system. However, he is generally free to do as he sees fit within the thicket of railroad rules. The locomotive is the prime mover of all rail traffic and the engineer is the prime controller of all distributive services on the railroad. He is responsible for making judgments concerning safe and efficient rail movements and for securing *rolling stock*—goods, passengers, and crew members.

In a recent noteworthy book on his specialty, industrial sociologist Richard Hall says the following of the craftsman in industry which he terms "the elite of blue-collar workers": "These occupations engage in manual rather than mental work . . ." (1975:187). Given the numerous codes of rules governing railroading, this certainly does not apply to the locomotive engineer. He is a mental worker par excellence, in addition to being a "manual operative" according to the terminology of sociology. The railway conductor is also a mental worker.

The locomotive engineer is a master operative, as is the airline pilot or the captain of a towboat for barges on an inland waterway. The engineer is in a craft occupation governed by a strong and venerable craft union (see Cook 1977). In their classic study entitled *Middletown,* Robert and Helen Lynd note that a tender of a machine for making glass bottles complained, "You can take a boy fresh from the farm and in three days he can manage a machine as well as I can, and I've been at it 27 years" (1929:74). Unlike the attendent of a machine used in mass production, it takes years to learn and perfect an engineer's skills: The hoghead is at the other end of the industrial occupational continuum.

Just how long does it take to train a locomotive engineer? No good answer has ever been reached. A minimum of three years of heavy and varied service coupled with considerable formal instruction is needed to make a qualified, but not well-seasoned, engineer. The National Transportation Safety Board said the following concerning a derailment of a difficult-to-control train operated by an engineer with four years of apprenticeship as a locomotive fireman and then three years experience as an engineer. "[H]is short experience raises the question of whether the engineer was capable of predicting the dynamic action of the train" (NTSB 1976:8). In my own survey research on the Western Division of the CC & U, I asked the following question:

"How much experience would it take to train a young man in engine service to equal you at your present level of skill and knowledge?"

One hundred and sixty-five out of 222 engine service employees completing the question answered, on the average, that it would take about 11.9 years.

Whatever the requisite duration of training, the hoghead has long been, and is generally regarded, as an adaptable, skilled, and responsible operator. As Charles Francis Adams, Jr., the railroad president of the Adams family, wrote a century ago:

> The intelligence, quickness of perception and capacity for taking care of themselves—that combination of qualities which, taken together, constitute individuality and adaptability to circumstance—vary greatly among the railroad employees of different countries. The American locomotive engineer, as he is called, is especially gifted in this way. He can be relied on to take care of himself and his train under circumstances which in other countries would be thought to insure disaster (Adams 1879a:592).

BECOMING A STUDENT

We will follow the early career of George Stone in order to give a tight illustrative focus to the "hiring out" of the typical engineman. Stone had no close relatives in railroading and none at all on the CC & U or its parent, the O & W. My survey research on the Western (Group A) and Eastern (Group B) Divisions of the CC & U and on a neighboring railroad district (C) shows the following in answer to the question: "Did a relative on this railroad in any way help or influence you in becoming an engineman?"

	Group A % (N)		Group B % (N)		Group C % (N)	
Yes	34.9	(64)	38.1	(16)	39	(16)
No	65.1	(121)	59.5	(25)	61	(25)

See the preface for additional information on the survey research.

Stone worked in a warehouse unloading boxcars and trucks upon graduation from high school, where he had earned a college prep diploma with good grades. He soon realized he was on the wrong side of the boxcar, so he contacted the road foreman of engines for each of the railroads in Urbana. The first one to respond, nine months later, was old Stan Layman of the CC & U. Stone assured Layman over the telephone that he had the necessary high school diploma and was eighteen years of age. Before giving notice at the warehouse, George put on his only suit, an exceedingly cheap one in which the threads disintegrated two years after its purchase, the better of his two pairs of shoes, and took the one-hour bus ride and two-mile walk to the roundhouse. Old Stan looked George over, asked him several questions concerning why he wanted to "hire out firing," and sent him off to a clerk (a male) in the superintendent's office who made an appointment with a company doctor for a physical examination.

A sign of our times is that educational requirements for entry into many jobs continue to rise. More and more jobs now require a high school diploma or a college degree; not so with engine service. The railroads presently continue a long-standing requirement of a high school diploma for entry into the craft of engine service. Earning a high school diploma gives reasonably good assurance of successful performance in learning the considerable tasks of an engineman (for example, training on the job and in a formal classroom), and in completion of the tasks (for example, reading and interpreting the myriad operating and other rules). Idiomatic command of English is needed for the learning and completion of work tasks and is necessary for effective communication with coworkers. Misunderstanding a written rule or a verbal command can be fatal. Formal training programs for locomotive engineers of the past few years have a technical level of instruction comparable to course work in junior colleges. Thus a competency level of a high-school graduate is necessary to enter engine service. Completion of high school courses and its four-year curriculum contribute to a person's development of self-esteem, self-discipline, confidence in assuming new and unfamiliar tasks, and conviction that tasks can be organized and completed by oneself within a narrowly bounded period of time.

A furloughed brakeman from a northeastern carrier was just ahead of Stone in the waiting room of the company "sawbones." He failed the physical because of postnasal drip. Stone felt he would never make it if the seasoned "brakie" could not. Stone gave urine and blood samples, was measured up and down, given a very thorough bodily examination, tested aurally, and made to jump about with his eyes closed while holding one foot. (Will I have to do this for a living, he thought.) Then the eye tests began: letter charts, charts with colored numbers hidden among colored dots, colored yarns, and colored lights viewed directly and as reflected from a mirror in a lighted and in a darkened room. Stone was given a completed form in a sealed envelope. The army-like physical was finished, but he would be periodically reexamined.

Back in Urbana Yard the clerk read the form and laconically told Stone: "You passed. See the Chief Crew Dispatcher." Walking over to the crew dispatcher's office, Stone marveled at the diesels being serviced by the hostlers, some only a few years older than himself. On storage tracks were several steam locomotives used as an emergency reserve for the normal locomotive pool at Urbana. Stone filled out forms, was given a stack of rule books and timetables, assigned to his first student trip, and told that a road foreman would examine him on operating and air brake rules at the end of his ten student trips. George was now a student fireman, the crew dispatcher told him. "Start reading your rule books," he was ordered.

Crew dispatchers have important informal functions. They dispense information about personal affairs of railroaders ("sand house gossip"), medical progress of ill or injured men, and planned and rumored changes in railroad operations, and generally serve as a clearinghouse for personal messages. They sometimes protect the men in various situations. For example, a member of a crew with an anxious wife might decide after getting off duty to stop off for a few beers on the way home. If asked to do so, the crew dispatcher will respond to a telephone inquiry of the wife by saying: "That's right Mizz White, job 34 hasn't tied up yet. Johnnie should be home in an hour or so. That's all right. Goodbye."

During the next few weeks, student Stone had to "write the book of rules" for a neighboring railroad over which he must qualify. Less enlightened than the CC & U, the other carrier requires that answers to questions on every operating rule be copied by hand from the rule book onto the blank spaces in a large workbook. Answers consist of all or most of a rule. The neighboring carrier apparently reasons that copying information, while the employee is uncompensated (on his own time), has something to do with the learning process. This survival from educational policy of the nineteenth century is one of many Victorian-era philosophies permeating American railroads today. Should Stone ever be charged with violating an operating rule on the neighboring carrier, say "getting a half a car-length by" a red stop and proceed signal before stopping with a heavy train, he would be shown in his own handwriting that the signal means "Stop; then proceed as prescribed by rule 291." He could then be fired or suspended from service, his own handwriting having helped convict him. "Isn't this rule 291 in your own hand?" he would be asked at an official investigation.

In the next few weeks, the company would question all of Stone's former employers with reference to his character and would especially check to see if he had a narcotics or other police record. Stone also filled out and signed a form for the company containing questions regarding his personal history. The form and its questions would have satisfied the F.B.I. Finally, Stone, with an armload of books and a head loaded with myriad pieces of new information, walked the two miles back to the bus stop.

The next day, Sunday, he arose at 4:00 A.M. He was to be a student fireman on the CX (Chicago Exchange) "leaving town" at 6:00 A.M. The crew consisted of "old heads" (rails with several decades of experience), who proved to be fairly friendly as well as instructive. New men are usually not talked to by older employees, except to tell them, tersely, what to do. Thus Stone would not always get such a positive reception, at least not until he had been on the job for several years. After "registering out" in the register book, Stone was instructed in the reading of the bulletin books and then taken over to the four-unit diesel idling on the outbound track amidst several other sets of units. The hoghead told Stone that as a railroader he was to expect a movement of rolling stock on any track in either direction at any time, thus forewarning him about complacency around track. The head brakeman showed Stone ("fireboy" as he called him) how to get on and off equipment

Electrical cables (above) and air hoses (below) connecting multiple units. Uncoupling levers link into top of "pin" entering the upper part of each coupler.

and especially to move backwards down ladders and steps on rolling stock. The head of a steel rail was never to be stepped upon, only across, to prevent slipping on its polished surface.

The fireman took Stone around the units for the then prescribed inspection. Back in the days of steam the division of labor had the fireman ("bakehead"/"tallowpot"/"smoke") do the inspection and preparation above the running board and the engineer below it. But in the diesel era, the fireman assumed the entire inspection. Below the running board of the four units, Stone checked for leaks onto the ground, loose brake rigging (he was to find this once in the next five years), proper positioning of *angle cocks* connecting the many air hoses between each unit (he was to find problems with these a few times), fuel in the sight glass on the belly fuel tank, and proper piston travel in the brake cylinders. This last was a frequent problem on locomotives and cars over the years. Climbing onto the running board of the last unit, he was shown how to "set" and "knock off" the hand brake found on every unit. He checked the engine room of each unit for oil leaks, noticed the lube oil and cooling water levels, and looked for proper operation of fuel pump via a sight glass. In the cab of each unit, he checked the position of circuit-breakers for the ON position, control switches to make sure the headlight circuit was cut through from the head to the rear end of all the units, and to make sure each unit was "on the line"—allowing it to develop electrical power. Stone was to find units not on line and without an established circuit to the rear headlight a number of times in the next few years.

In more recent years, the company has instructed engine crews not to inspect units prior to departure in an effort to reduce labor costs. The men's attitude now is, "If the company doesn't care, why should I? Let the units burn up or run out of fuel." In a similar effort to reduce labor costs some time after Stone hired out, the company had the hostlers take the units from the departure track and put them on the train and had a crew dispatcher drive the crew from the register room to the units on the train. Still more recently, the company is back to having the crew step outside the register room, walk a few feet (while informally glancing at the brake cylinders) to the units, and then take them to their train, as Clint Johnson did in Chapter 1. Similarly, the company cannot make up its managerial mind as to whether or not units sitting in the terminal area waiting for servicing or the day's assignment should have their diesel engines shut down or left idling. The policy has literally been on again, off again.

Stone was ready for his first "road trip" on the CX with four 1500 h.p. units and 5000 trailing tons. Additionally, they would need a helper locomotive to get over the Maxwell Pass. Stone would make additional student trips on through freights and local branch line freights, one yard engine, and one helper locomotive pushing trains over mountain grades. He would be a student officially for only the next two weeks until he had satisfactorily taken his student trips, passed his preliminary examinations, and finally "made his [seniority] date" (working the first trip as a regular fireman at regular wages). However, as is customary, he would be referred to as a student by the other railroaders for about a year.

Sometimes there is a long duration between the completion of all formal student requirements and the making of the date because the company likes to have a large pool of qualified applicants. In the 1950s and 1960s the waiting period was a few months to a year. Stone was lucky as he was an early bird. Two men with railroad connections and two without made their date before him that year, and *seventy* followed him. It was a boom year, and traffic mushroomed on the CC & U following a recession year in which no student firemen or brakemen and only a few student switchmen were hired. Interestingly, on the day Stone made his all-important seniority date, June 1, he actually slept round the clock to recuperate from several sixteen-hour freight trips, plus travel to terminals, and from studying his rule books in any spare hours. He really made his first "pay trip" on a night switch engine on June 2. It was almost unheard of for the company to make a mistake on a seniority date. After making his date, Stone would have a period of six months in which to "get over the derail." During this period the company kept him on probation for six months and could dismiss him without cause. (Today the time is three months.) Once over the derail, he would have union representation to protect him and, additionally, could be used as a fireman on a passenger train.

Upon making his date, Stone purchased one of several varieties of officially authorized watches of railroad grade. The watch serves as a badge of office of a rail, and its use while on duty is required of operating employees. Company officers check watches from time to time to insure that they do not vary more than 30 seconds from standard time as prescribed by operating rules 1, 2, and 3.

Stone had hired out on the railroad for a number of reasons, including interest in railroading, salary, and disinterest in a job that confined him to a desk or a workbench. His reasons seem to parallel those of other railroaders. On a five point scale ranging from 1 to 5, 1 (strongly agree), 2 (agree), 3 (undecided), 4 (disagree), and 5 (strongly disagree), the enginemen of groups A, B, and C scored the following when answering parts of the overall question, "What led you to become an engineman?":

	Group A	Group B	Group C
(a) security	1.97	1.69	1.80
(b) steam locomotives	2.11	2.03	2.43
(c) monthly earnings	2.04	1.65	1.84
(d) railroading in general	2.00	1.69	2.05
(e) engineman's prestige	2.67	1.97	2.88

For further information on survey research used in this book see the preface.

Generally, rails like railroading as a career and, more specifically, the freedom that it gives them on the job. This is especially so for enginemen. The reaction to the survey research statement "I have plenty of opportunity on the job to use my own judgment" is as follows:

Group A	Group B	Group C
2.16	2.12	2.45

Reaction to the statement "My work is enjoyable, that is, apart from consideration of wages, railroading is interesting and pleasurable" is:

Group A	Group B	Group C
2.13	1.95	1.88

Enginemen generally work on a railroad without any thought of being promoted up from the ranks into the positions of company officers. Many think that rails who are promoted have connections. With regard to the survey statement "An engineman has a real chance to be promoted to company officer" the reaction is a negative one, more so for the men of the CC & U at Urbana, Group A:

Group A	Group B	Group C
4.11	3.90	3.40

And "Promotion to the rank of company officer usually depends upon having relatives or close friends among present officers":

Group A	Group B	Group C
2.22	2.56	2.32

Importance of enginemen in railroading is generally recognized, with some modesty, by these men: "Employees in engine service are the most essential employees in railroading":

Group A	Group B	Group C
1.78	1.83	1.93

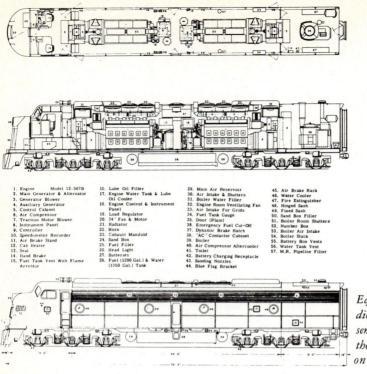

1. Engine Model 12-567B	16. Lube Oil Filler	29. Main Air Reservoir	45. Air Brake Rack
2. Main Generator & Alternator	17. Engine Water Tank & Lube Oil Cooler	30. Air Intake & Shutters	46. Water Cooler
3. Generator Blower		31. Boiler Water Filler	47. Fire Extinguisher
4. Auxiliary Generator	18. Engine Control & Instrument Panel	32. Engine Room Ventilating Fan	48. Hinged Sash
5. Control Cabinet		33. Air Intake For Grids	49. Fixed Sash
6. Air Compressor	19. Load Regulator	34. Fuel Tank Gauge	50. Sand Box Filler
7. Traction Motor Blower	20. 34" Fan & Motor	35. Door (Plain)	51. Boiler Room Shutters
8. Instrument Panel	21. Radiator	36. Emergency Fuel Cut-Off	52. Number Box
9. Controller	22. Horn	37. Dynamic Brake Hatch	53. Boiler Air Intake
10. Speedometer Recorder	23. Exhaust Manifold	38. "AC" Contactor Cabinet	54. Boiler Stack
11. Air Brake Stand	24. Sand Box	39. Boiler	55. Battery Box Vents
12. Cab Heater	25. Fuel Filler	40. Air Compressor Aftercooler	56. Water Tank Vent
13. Seat	26. Head Light	41. Toilet	57. M.R. Pipeline Filter
14. Hand Brake	27. Batteries	42. Battery Charging Receptacle	
15. Fuel Tank Vent With Flame Arrestor	28. Fuel (1200 Gal.) & Water (1350 Gal.) Tank	43. Sanding Nozzles	
		44. Blue Flag Bracket	

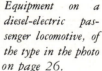

Equipment on a diesel-electric passenger locomotive, of the type in the photo on page 26.

EXAMINING THE DIESEL-ELECTRIC

Fireman Stone learned a considerable amount about diesel-electric locomotives during his student days, examining them while on runs and when visiting engine houses in his spare time. What he learned about steam locomotives may be of interest to some readers of this book, but will not be recounted as it is not directly germane to contemporary railroading. A small percentage of locomotives used in North America is (straight) electric. What will be said about diesels generally applies to them, except that their prime mover is not a component engine but a power station that supplies electricity through overhead lines or third rails. For information on the diesel-electric locomotives as a work environment see Gamst 1975a, 1975c.

As I have discussed at length elsewhere (Gamst 1975c), almost all locomotives in North American service since 1960 are diesel-electrics in which a diesel engine drives a main generator which produces electricity to power electric traction motors, one of which is geared to each axle of the locomotive. At the engineer's control stand in the cab (see page 8), after the proper setting of various switches and levers and as the throttle is advanced from idle position to positions run-1 through run-8, the main generator is electrically connected to the traction motors through an electrical control cabinet. With each throttle advance the engine increases its r.p.m.s, delivering more mechanical power to the generator which then furnishes more electrical power to the motors propelling the locomotive. Thus, each railway diesel is in reality a diesel-electric powerhouse on wheels. Dr. Rudolf Diesel, the German inventor of the diesel engine late in the nineteenth century, could foresee the use of his invention in a rationalization of railroading (Diesel 1894):

> We consider the new [engine] especially applicable to railways, to replace ordinary steam locomotives, not only on account of its great economy of fuel, but because there is no boiler. In fact the day may possibly come when it may completely change the present system of steam locomotion on existing lines of rails.

Stone learned not just about propulsion of locomotives but about braking as well. Many diesels, including those in mountain service, are equipped with a *dynamic brake,* a system in which the traction motors and the generator exciter are connected electrically to retard the locomotive and its train. The motors are electrically reconnected from the control stand (through low voltage circuits in the control cabinet) as electric generators which produce power dissipated as heat in roof-mounted resistor grids cooled by a fan. In this way the momentum of a moving unit is converted to electrical power, a process which consumes the rotating mechanical energy of the axles and thus retards movement. Locomotives of all kinds have an automatic air brake system (for use of air brakes on locomotives and cars) and an independent air brake system (for use of locomotive brakes independently of automatic [all-of-train] brakes). The automatic feature of the former system is that if the *brake pipe* (also called *train line*) of the brake system running the length of a train should break, burst, or separate the brakes will apply automatically.

Train handling, the coordinated use in the locomotive cab of throttle and dynamic brake in conjunction with the two air brake systems, requires considerable skill—even more so in mountainous territory. Stone hoped to be referred to some day as an "air man," one who has a much better than average grasp of the considerable skill of train handling. The skill does not come easily and involves a good amount of practical experience, getting into particular problems, study of mechanical and air brake rules, and the instruction given by veteran engineers. Informal exchange of information with coworkers about operating problems and trouble shooting on locomotives enhances the breadth of experience of any one individual. Exchange takes place in the cab, register room, and during layover at terminals away from home. Above all, Stone learned that he should always know whether his train had its slack stretched or bunched prior to braking or accelerating. Such practice prevented him from pulling a train apart with his powerful units or from causing a harmful run-in of the slack which could damage cargo and injure the crew members on the caboose. Through time, Stone would learn a considerable amount about the care and feeding of diesel-electrics.

LEARNING THE CRAFT

Stone soon realized that all firemen not only learn the duties of the fireman, generally assisting the engineer, by maintaining power output on locomotives, but are also in training as engineers-to-be. Firemen are officially termed "locomotive firemen-helpers." Their occupational education has traditionally been on-the-job instruction and practical experience under the tutelage of engineers. Further brief instruction is given bi-annually in classroom cars called "rules cars" and irregularly and informally in various places by a road foreman of engines. Firemen learn when asked questions by another fireman and especially by self-study of various rulebooks, textbooks, and question and answer booklets prepared by both a particular carrier and by commercial firms. This entire traditional method of education is inefficient, and often takes place in part by what appears to be a kind of pedagogical osmosis. Depending upon circumstance, some men have more opportunity to learn quicker and better than others.

Recently, the carriers have instituted an apprentice program for locomotive engineers. In this program, newly hired employees in the craft of engine service become firemen for only a short while and then are sent to an engineer training school where extensive formal instruction is given in the classroom, in mechanical repair shops, and in the cab. The apprentice engineers then receive further practical experience under the guidance of veteran engineers on their home district. After they pass appropriate written and oral examinations, they formally become locomotive engineers, receiving a second seniority date, as engineer, on the joint engineers' and firemen's seniority roster for a particular seniority district.

The difference between fireman and engineer is not absolute, as Stone soon ascertained. Employment as engineer, as opposed to fireman-helper or even being furloughed (temporarily laid off), depends upon the number of assignments generated by the amount of rail traffic flowing over the district. In the great Depression, it was said that there were two engineers in every cab (no fireman unpromoted to engineer) and two conductors in every caboose (no brakeman unpromoted to conductor). In times of normal cyclical reduction of traffic, senior men "bump" (take the assignments) of junior men. Because of such bumping, many of the "younger" brakemen and firemen are furloughed by the carrier, while some engineers and conductors are back in assignments for engine and ground crews as firemen and brakemen. As business increases on the district, the carrier "force-assigns," according to rank of seniority, the engineers holding the senior most firemen's assignments so that they are placed in the junior most, least desirable, engineer's assignments. As the senior fireman is "forced" onto one of the worst jobs for engineers, all men younger than he can eventually bid up the job ladder because of the vacancy left by the senior man. Not all junior men avail themselves of this opportunity to change jobs. Life on the railroad means bidding up and being bumped down the parallel job ladders for firemen and engineers.

Seniority, in labor relations, is an employee's length of employment with a firm or a subunit of it and is used as a basis for rates of pay, assignment to jobs, order of furlough and recall, promotion, and other aspects of job status. In railroading, seniority allows a man or woman to work in a particular craft on a designated district (engine service on the Eastern Division of the CC &

U). Seniority lists are maintained and posted by the carrier. Seniority positions of two individuals are sometimes exchanged between districts but not between crafts.

Fireman Stone thought it somewhat amusing that he would steadily increase in seniority through the kind of jobs he could hold (generally: night yard engine, afternoon yard engine, daylight yard engine, local freight and mountain helper locomotive service, through freight, and finally through passenger service) only to be "promoted" to an engineer on a low-paying night yard engine with a second, similar ascent of a parallel job ladder. Deaths, disabilities, retirements, and other terminations would gradually push him up the ladders, but at the same time technological change and other rationalization of work would constantly lessen the number of rungs on the ladders. Apropos of this, Stone would often hear other enginemen say, "The old heads take their seniority with them when they retire."

Firemen, past and present, are required to study for and to take promotion exams to become engineers, but brakemen are not required to become conductors. Because of the interrelated nature of the occupational positions of fireman and engineer, it is appropriate to consider them socially as having one general occupational status of engineman (engine service employee) with two specific statuses, of fireman and of engineer-fireman. A fireman who has been promoted to engineer but who is not holding an engineer's assignment is called a "promoted man" to distinguish him from ordinary firemen.

FLATTENING WHEELS

Early in his career, Stone learned that one of the worst sins committed by an engineman was "flattening an engine," or making "square wheels" through improper handling of the air brakes. Too great of an independent brake application, especially on slippery rail, causes the iron brake shoes to seize the steel wheels of a locomotive, thereby making *flat spots* on the tread of the wheel as it slides on the steel rail. Not only did the company add disciplinary demerits to one's personal record for such a mishap, but other rails joked about and ridiculed those who had more than a few of these calamities. One older fireman was always plagued with the name "Flat Wheel" Carson. Some of the senior, hard-bitten hogheads would not let him run the engine on the main line. Many engineers would have their fireman enter the stock words "old flat spots" onto the daily locomotive inspection report, mandatory under federal law, thus protecting themselves from any company inquiry into the small one-quarter to one-half inch scuff marks found on the wheels of some yard locomotives. The "clomping" sound of a locomotive with flat spots in excess of one inch is referred to as the "walking" of the unit. "Old Flat Wheel flattened the 1338 so bad that you could hear it walking before you could see it coming," related a vexed hoghead eating his meal in a local "beanery." A waggish remark often runs, "Some of those 'old flat spots' sound nearly new."

Stone experienced three flattening incidents, all of which further enculturated him into the rail world. The first was during the month after he had made his seniority date as fireman and was just beginning the customary informal instruction in the running of a night switch locomotive in Urbana Yard. After completing the switching of cars for several outbound freights, the yardmaster had Stone, who was running the engine under the supervision of engineer Roger Feranti, go to the adjacent rip yard—a yard where freight cars are repaired and serviced. Oil spills onto the tracks in the course of such work. While "spotting" (positioning) boxcars needing servicing on the greasy track, Stone noticed that the drive wheels on the 125-ton yard locomotive made a scuffing sound during braking, instead of the normal squeal of the steel wheels being retarded by the iron brake shoes. Feranti yelled, "You're picking up the drivers!" The words, though heard, were as incomprehensible to Stone as the scuffing noise. Feranti, standing on the open rear deck of the unit, was leaning out and observing ahead to make sure Stone understood the lantern signals of the switchmen, who were spotting cars at worksites having only a few inches of tolerance for a car's position. By the time Feranti flew in through the rear cab door and pulled the independent brake valve into quick release position, it was too late; the 1340 had one-and-one-quarter inch flat spots.

Stone walked the 1340 all over the yard that night and even carmen and yard clerks turned their heads and smiled as they watched him pass by. "Never again," thought Stone. Feranti, negotiating with the yardmaster and a roundhouse supervisor, had special abrasive brake shoes put on the 1340. The special brake shoes are painted a bright, ignominious red that seemed to glow in even the dimmest recess of the dark yard. Stone noticed that the red shoes were audibly different from the regular ones. He could almost feel their very presence on the locomotive he was running. The unit was kept in the outbound yard until the flat spots were worn down to one-half inch. Nothing was ever recorded concerning the incident.

The second incident was with engineer Greer in the steeply graded River Yard in Urbana. Student Stone had a full year of solid experience working on seven-day-a-week yard engines and on the *extra board,* a rotating working list protecting recently vacated, new, and special assignments. Greer was confident when Stone coupled to the long cut of heavily laden freight cars that his fireman would charge the brake system, leave River Yard, run along the main line, and enter the inbound yard of the Urbana Yard, all without incident. Greer was correct. Stone did have the air brake skill and experience for the run; but he did not have the experience to deal with the defective equipment on the 1308. The yardmaster, coming in on the cab radio, said he needed many of the "hot" cars in their train right away. Greer told Stone to finish charging his brake system as he rolled out to the main line signal about one-half mile distant on a downgrade. Stone would control the speed with the locomotive brakes alone until the cars were fully charged. Stone extinguished his cablights and signaled with his headlight to move ahead. The head end switchman motioned him to come ahead and then climbed onto the first car behind the 1308 as it rolled past.

Stone had noticed that all the air brake gauge lights were inoperative that night. He did not notice until too late that when placed in *lap* position the independent brake valve leaked air into the locomotive's brake cylinders until an unintended full locomotive brake application was made. (Lap on a brake valve ceases further applications of braking force and holds what has previously been applied.) Rolling downgrade out of River Yard toward the *derail* that guarded the exit to the yard, Stone bunched his cars with the independent brake valve by lapping off about 15 p.s.i. pressure in his locomotive brake cylinders, out of the total possible of 40 p.s.i. Not being able to read his gauge lights, Stone did not realize that he soon had all 40 p.s.i. gradually leaked into the cylinders. His speed had picked up only slightly beyond his original 6 m.p.h.

Entering downgrade onto the outbound track leading to the main line, Stone expected and saw the violet lens gleaming menacingly on the derailing switch that opposed his movement. Stone moved his brake valve slowly from lap to application for another 10 p.s.i., thereby attempting to retard his cars still further in the normal way. Nothing happened. He flipped on the bright cab lights, diminishing his night vision, and saw that he had all 40 p.s.i. in his cylinders. He was now almost upon the derail and the switchman was just alighting from the ladder of the first boxcar behind the 1308 to go and throw the derail into the clear position. A normal service application of the train brakes with a not completely charged brake system would not take hold in time. Quickly, Stone pulled the automatic brake valve from *running,* and charging, all the way over to *emergency* position. Exhausting out of an emergency orifice under each car, compressed air whooshed onto the ground the entire length of the train. Forward motion began to slow but the switchman was not quite to the derail yet. Stone had only one action left. He let the locomotive brakes build up to 70 p.s.i. of emergency pressure. He intended to bleed off the pressure slightly as they ground to a halt, thus keeping the wheels from sliding. Unfortunately, the two forward pairs of drive wheels picked up and slid flat just before a stop was made right in front of the derail.

Afterward, Stone was furious with himself because he had caused large one-inch flat spots, even though he was told nothing would be put on record considering the condition of the gauge lights and the leaking brake valve, both of which were soon repaired. Not one person taunted him when they heard of the circumstances. "You were set up to be shoved through the derail by the cars," he was told by an old switchman, "so you're lucky to only have a few square wheels." Greater experience on his part would probably have prevented Stone from flattening the 1308. He would never again accept or operate an engine without gauge lights. But, he did at other times run with partially charged cars in order to keep certain yardmasters happy. In other words, he would play with fire, but would be more familiar with the dangers. The yardmaster wielded both carrot and stick. He dispensed "early quits" and the preferred tasks in the greater terminal area, but he could also hand out irksome chores.

The third incident took place three years after Stone made his date as fireman. It was 7:30 A.M. and his eyes itched from a long night of peering at switchmen's signals. Coming out of a long industrial spur in an alley bisected by a major city street, Stone kept his speed down to 4 m.p.h. with ten loads behind him on the very slight downgrade. The two switchmen on the crew flagged the crossing, stopped all the traffic with their bodies, and then signaled Stone that it was all right to continue rolling out of the alley and across the six-lane street. As his 1325 approached the crossing with whistle sounding and bell on, an old battered auto ran along the curb lane in order to pass on the right of the heavy traffic stopped for the train. The auto then halted upon the tracks of the grade crossing because stopped vehicles blocked all lanes beyond the crossing. It rested at the mouth of the alley, just 40 feet beyond the slowly rolling 1325 (125 tons) and its ten loads (about 700 tons).

Stone immediately turned on the rail sanders to gain adhesion on the poor, slippery rail of the old spur and applied all the brakes by putting the automatic brake valve in *service* (application) position. He could feel the locomotive drive wheels begin to pick up and slide with only 25 p.s.i. in the locomotive brake cylinders. Now, instinctively, Stone put the locomotive brakes into quick release and recovered the free rolling of the wheels, but lost the considerable braking power of the 1325. The boxcars' brakes began slowly to retard the forward motion of the train, and the front coupler of the 1325 stopped about two feet from the right-hand doors of the auto. By then its seven passengers were scrambling out the other side.

The first two times that he had flattened wheels Stone had been forgiven by managers and his peers because of the circumstances—a brand new student at the throttle and defective equipment. He most likely would be allowed no further "alibis" and he would seek no more.

The grizzled yard conductor of the Violent Alley job, as it was called, summed up Stone's thoughts when he came in to the cab after they had reached the main line. "That silly son-of-a-bitch was so frightened that he must have shit in his pants before he jumped out the door. That's the last time he'll pull that stunt when a crossing is being flagged. I'm glad that you had sense enough, Georgie, not to pick up the drivers and flatten the engine on his account. Better to flatten his ass than the engine."

George Stone was no longer considered a student but he was still learning technical skills and being enculturated by his fellow rails in the rather closed society of the rail world. His value system was still being formed; some of it on an unconscious level. Old heads no longer called him "you" or "student." A diminutive form of his first name was now used and would stick with him all of his career. Still others who were accepted by the rails would be labeled with less pleasant sounding names, but which were nonetheless affectionate: Hee Haw, Balloon Head, Bull Ape, Killer, Chippie, Studs, and so forth.

LEARNING, A RETROSPECTION

The learning experienced by enginemen may be classified into at least four broad areas. The first is manual operative skills coupled with technical knowledge. Examples include operating by hand the track switches on the main line which are also remote controlled or electrically locked, operating the automatic air brake system on a mountain downgrade when the dynamic brake is malfunctioning, rerailing a car that has left the rails, or restoring power in a unit after its red, yellow, blue, and white color coded warning lights have come on while an alarm bell rings furiously. These are learned manual skills acquired by coordinated reflection upon oral instruction, demonstration on the job, and all-important reading of the appropriate information.

The second area is codified knowledge of rules and guidelines for operating procedures. It comes from intensive study, practical application, and constant interpretation and restudy of various written sources: the operating rule book, mechanical and air brake rule book, labor contract, timetable, bulletins, and so forth. In a particular situation, What am I required to do? What should I do? What must I do?

The third area is on-the-job judgment, apart from the skills noted in the previous two areas. This area cannot be readily taught and cannot always be easily learned. When will moving cars clear the running track during switching so that another car may be "kicked" (propelled by momentum after being released from a locomotive that has been slowed) past it? How soon should I cycle the automatic air brakes on a downgrade without diminishing the supply of compressed air at a faster rate than it can be replenished? How close on the time of a following train does one run without delaying it? Only the

Great skill and judgment demonstrated by switchman, who guided boxcar down a track on a hill to coupling with waiting locomotive. Man has his eye on closing gap between car and engine couplers as he makes final adjustment on the wheel of the hand brake.

knowledge of experience and a knack for accurate judgment are of value in this area.

The fourth area is learning the railroaders' code of etiquette. Here a rail internalizes the mores or values governing interpersonal relations within the railroad social system. How should I act and speak without becoming offensive to my fellow rails? How should I behave as a rail without risking being derided or even shunned? A man may be good in area one but not in two. Three may be mastered only somewhat and four may be partially beyond his comprehension. A good rail excels in all four areas.

4/Operating and other rules

In this chapter we learn of codified sets of regulations that guide the behavior of rails on and off the job. Ethnologists want to know why it is that people act and say things as they do and what the range of variation is from their modal behavior. Central to the work of rails is what is known to them as "the rules." Many hundreds of these exist in complex and interrelated codes for train operations, mechanical and air brake practices, safety on the job, and even activity away from work. Thus, when answering the above traditional ethnological query with regard to the rails, "the rules" are elemental to an understanding of what they do, say, and think.

Most railroads have their central rules in a book of operating rules and additionally in one on air brake and mechanical rules. Supplemental rules of these kinds are found in the operating timetable, which, in turn is updated by new and changed rules posted in books as *Timetable/Superintendent's Bulletins*. Notices and circulars containing operating instructions are issued and posted in separate books by authority below the level of the *division superintendent*. The agreement, or labor contract, between each craft and a carrier has hundreds of regulations, many of which affect operations, for example, when and how long can a crew stop for a meal? The most particularized instructions are the *clearances, train orders,* and operating messages issued to a given train by the train dispatcher. These provide for stipulated movement on main tracks to certain stations at designated times, and the passing or meeting of various trains in specified ways.

THE BOOK OF RULES

Student Stone carries a small book while on duty. He reads it both on and off duty and from a distance he appears rather like one of the devout reading the good book. The volume found in Stone's hands so frequently is one furnishing material for lively discussions among railroaders. It is, about four-by-six inches, contains about 200 pages, and is the focal point of the operations of each railroad. Usually its title is *Rules of the Operating Department* or *Operating Rules,* but in the nineteenth century it was often, *Rules and Regulations.* No matter which title, it is always called the "book of rules" by rails. Other books of regulations exist but the book of rules is central and fundamental to the everyday business of railroading. The book may be considered the Bible of railroading, its blueprint for operations, and its very soul. As General Rule A states at the beginning of any rule book: "A. Employees whose duties are prescribed by these rules must provide themselves with a copy." This current prime rule differs little from a rule in the 1839 *Rules and Regulation-book* of the pioneer Liverpool and Manchester Railway of Britain: "N.B.—Every overlooker, engineman, guard [brakeman], policeman, and gateman employed in the Liverpool and Manchester Railway, shall keep a copy of these rules constantly on his person, under a penalty of a fine of five shillings" (Whishaw 1842:217). Operating rules in the United States and Canada have their origin in British rules of these kinds and many today are easily recognizable descendants of rules in the pioneering British codes and of operating conditions that first obtained on these early carriers.

Any of the numerous numbered operating rules and lettered sections of these usually cannot be understood in isolation from the other rules, which are systemic and combine to guide railroad operations in a manner not conveyed by a single rule. For example, rule 17 reads:

> Headlight must be displayed, burning bright to the front of every train by day and night. It must be extinguished when a train has stopped clear of main track to meet a train, or is standing to meet a train at the end of double track or at a junction.

Thus the locomotive headlight is not merely a means of illumination or a warning device for alerting people to a train movement. As stated by the rules, it is a basic train signal indicating that a main track is occupied or perhaps fouled in some way, by a derailed car, shifted lading, or the rear end of a long train hanging out of a side track onto the main track. On the very common single-track lines, when the crew of a train approaches another having its headlight on bright, it proceeds, as required by rule, with great caution, crawling along prepared to stop within the distance seen to be free of obstruction or faulty track. A number of other rules concerning train order operations, flagging protection, and movement of trains come into play should the approaching train have to stop, because of conditions or lack of information, after seeing an opposing headlight burning.

Discussions of operating rules among rails have many of them acting as "rules experts" or "switch shanty lawyers," who are well informed on the intricacies of the rules. One source of prestige among rails is to be truly conversant with the operating rules and their interrelated implications yet not be ostentatious in displaying knowledge of rules. Because members of rail crews are necessarily largely unsupervised, and thus men may work for a year or more without carrier officers present on their runs, they must refer to the published operating rules for guidance in meeting the changing, novel operating situations that constantly confront them. Sometimes the exacting systemic rules are not consulted as they must be at the time of a novel situation and the consequences can be extremely dangerous, as will be seen with the case of running against the current of traffic from J N Tower.

SCOPE OF THE RULES

Requirements of the operating rules govern almost all conditions for movement of trains and locomotives, use of other equipment, and behavior on the job. To some extent, the rules also regulate the lives and mold the personalities of rails (Cottrell 1939; Kemnitzer 1977) who must, according to the rules, "reside where required by the management, and comply with instructions from proper authority." Further they must not "engage in other business without proper authority" and, highly important, "An employee subject to call must not absent himself from his usual calling place without notice to those required to call him." This last rule means that many rails must live within earshot of the telephone and are virtual prisoners in their own homes for large periods of time.

Railroads have not yet entirely left the early Victorian and pre-Victorian era of industrial personnel relations which are quite militaristic and authoritarian. The carriers have all-encompassing umbrella rules which allow them to enforce what their managers believe (or hope?) is moral and nondeviant behavior among rails. To varying degrees, the managers may not themselves be so early Victorian in outlook before they begin to manage for the carriers, but they at least verbalize and to some extent internalize the outlook as they enter the managerial social setting. Perhaps certain varieties of authoritarian personalities are preadapted for railroad management and are selected when managers choose new managers as peers. The managerial subculture of railroading allows the survival of patterns of culture which are somewhat analogous to living fossils in the organic realm of nature. (Survivals of earlier patterns of culture into a later time has been a concern of anthropology for over a century [Gamst and Norbeck 1976:34,40–41].)

Much of the wordage and surviving intent of umbrella rules for conduct are managerial "dinosaurs" from a bygone era which we would ordinarily encounter only in the documents of the historical record of the industrial revolution. Behavioral umbrella rules in railroading are anachronistic survivals from times when country folk had to be made to conform to the "new discipline" of industry and its captains (cf. Ashton 1969:85). The "discipline" was the forced conditioning of green workers to the rhythm of the machine and to the synchronization of the clock and was as important a part of early industrialization as were technologic innovations. An important general umbrella rule in railroading runs:

> Employees will not be retained in the service who are careless of the safety of themselves or others, insubordinate, dishonest, immoral, quarrelsome or otherwise vicious, or who do not conduct themselves in such a manner that the railroad will not be subjected to criticism and loss of good will, or who do not meet their personal obligations.

In short, a rail must be a perfect Victorian trooper or he will be cashiered out of the regiment. Instead of having his sword and epaulets taken away, he is required to turn in his large brass key for locks on company equipment, and his book of rules. In the Victorian manner, it follows that, "When passing through dining cars while patrons are being served, train employees, other than those collecting transportation, must remove their caps." Rails joke about these rules for their deportment and they also resent them.

The waggish test for whether or not a rail is "otherwise vicious" is said to be if he actually "foams at the mouth" when he becomes angry. Many yard-masters are rumored to become rabidly vicious when things go wrong, as they often do. It is said that at such times a yardmaster "foams at the mouth" and, after depressing the buttons to activate all of his loudspeakers, he "screams and hollers something awful"; that is, "enough to make a grown man blush" with embarassment at the vicious language. The account that follows is a good and telling example of the "vicious" behavior which management's umbrella rule attempts to control.

A yardmaster once became rabidly vicious regarding the actions of a student ground crew. One clear, crisp evening, while working an extra assignment, Stone found himself on the 1307, with a green crew consisting of two switch-men and a yard conductor. The three groundmen were inexperienced in gen-eral and, in particular, had no knowledge of the River Yard with its steep gradient. The 1307 left the main Urbana yards in a hurry, propelled by the voice-over-the-loudspeaker of a grizzled senior yardmaster, named Lawrence. He needed two recently loaded cars of valuable freight for the FM (Fast Merchandise) scheduled to leave Urbana at 8:00 P.M. It was then 6:00 P.M. and already dark, but all the 1307 had to do was run a few miles down the main line, go into the River Yard, get the two "hot" cars from their respec-tive tracks, and "dash home" to Lawrence. The ground crew of the 1307 nor-mally switched cars right under the yardmaster's watchful eyes on the upper end of the outbound yard, but this particular night all of the yard engines with experienced ground crews were occupied with more involved tasks.

The 1307 coupled to the first "hot" load (of ice cream cones), standing on a holding track, without incident and then ran downgrade on the long running track of River Yard until it came to the spur leading to the Acme Freight Forwarding Company. The car of cones was uncoupled in the clear, on the running track, above the spur; one of its wheels was blocked with a small piece of wood, as is customary. The 1307 then moved ahead past the spur's track switch, which was thrown, and backed into Acme spur number 1 to get the furthermost of five cars loaded with boxed general merchandise. The inex-perienced switchmen began motioning the 1307 back, thus coupling in turn each of the five separated cars so that the end car could be set out of the spur against the car of cones, and the others returned to their spots. The switch-men did not notice the long steel platform extending through the open doors on either side of the fourth car into a car spotted opposite it on a parallel track (Acme spur 2). Stone could not see what was ahead of the first car because of the curvature of the two parallel spurs filled with cars. As is customary, he continued to act upon lantern signals to "come back" slowly after each car was coupled. As he coupled the third car into the fourth, he heard the clank of steel and instantly received three stop signals from the lanterns of the ground-men. It would be some time before car four was freed from the jammed plat-form so that car five could be taken away.

Several minutes later, in an unrelated incident, the carload of ice cream cones overcame the resistance of the apparently too-small wooden wedge under the forward wheel. The car was pulled downgrade by gravity, over the splin-tered wedge and through the track switch, which was still lined for the Acme spur. The wheels of the forty-ton load bent the switch so that it could not be thrown either way. The 1307 was trapped and the fifth Acme boxcar thus was doubly trapped. The ice cream cone load was now on the wrong side of the 1307 and was rolling away rapidly. A switchman dropped his lantern, streaked after the car, mounted it, and stopped it with its hand brake just before it ran through the derailing switch with its violet signal light at the base of the running track. The derail protected the main line from such mis-haps in River Yard. If the car's hand brake had not been on the end nearest to the switchman, he could never have mounted and stopped the load in time to prevent it from derailing, turning over on its side, and destroying many tons of ice cream cones. "I just made 500,000 kids happy," he said after saving the car.

"Yeah, but Lawrence won't be happy," said another switchman.

After a while, Yardmaster Lawrence called over the radio: "Come in 1307. Do you *have* the cars? What's keeping you?"

Stone answered the radio and explained that the cars had them, rather than the other way around. He gave all the nasty details to Lawrence. It was 7:05 P.M. and the FM would soon be capped with its caboose. Its crew had been called thirty-five minutes ago and the hostler was setting out the diesel units which would pull it, minus the two hot loads, to the east.

"JESUS CHRIST!!! What is the matter with you Goddamn, stupid bas-tards?" the yardmaster screamed over the radio. (One rule says, "No employee shall . . . utter any obscene, indecent or profane language via radio.")

The FM left Urbana Yard without the two hot cars and Lawrence was indeed very rabid. "Maybe we should call the superintendent and tell him we have a *vicious* employee here in the yard office," a switchman cracked to a yard clerk.

"Yeah, the old man [superintendent] will have to get a gun to shoot Lawrence, from the sound of things," the clerk replied.

Many of the men believe that the rule prohibiting "otherwise vicious" be-havior is an anachronism from earlier times when the carriers actively combat-ted labor union activities of their employees. The company does not need to use the rule on vicious behavior, men on the CC & U agree, because infraction of almost any rule can be used as a pretext for severe discipline. Yet this rule and other general umbrella rules on personal behavior remain in the latest revisions of operating codes.

General rule G exercises still more control over the lives of rails. It now reads, "the use of alcoholic beverages or narcotics by employees subject to duty is prohibited." (Virtually no rails use narcotics save for tobacco and coffee.) Until a few years ago, rule G read, "the use of intoxicants or narcotics is prohibited." After the turn of the century the rule read: "The use of intoxicants by employees while on duty is prohibited. Their habitual use, or the frequenting of places where they are sold, is sufficient cause for dismissal."

The intent of the earliest rule prevailed until recently, when the carriers finally realized they could no longer prevent employees from drinking in public after they had gone off duty. Prior to this time, engineer Glover was arrested by the Jackson police allegedly for being publicly intoxicated, and this event was noted in the Jackson newspaper. The CC & U fired Glover for his deportment even though he was not subject to call for duty at the time of the incident. Many months afterward, the carrier reinstated Glover. Today, management most likely would not try to control the off-duty behavior of an employee in this heavy-handed way. Glover had been punished by the municipality of Jackson and exposed by the press for what many would consider a slight offense, if any. Adding insult to injury, the carrier deprived him of his livelihood. To say the least, Glover was dismayed when company officers pulled the economic rug out from under his feet.

LOCAL ADDITIONS TO RULES

Books of rules are not supposed to be absolutely uniform across the United States, conforming to *The Standard Code of Operating Rules* of the American Association of Railroads (1965). The rule books of each carrier differ somewhat in their wording and local intent. Additionally, the operating rules of each railroad are modified in three ways, causing much further variation than is apparent from cursory comparison of the various books of rules.

Permanent operating rules peculiar to a particular railroad division are additions to or modifications of a carrier's version of the standard code. These are found in employees' operating timetables and attached special rules, which are published in pamphlet form and reissued from once every few months to once every few years. Superintendent's bulletins and other notices posted in a bulletin book may amend the operating rules and timetable rules on a few hours' notice. Local custom in operating procedures modifies the above kinds of printed operating rules still further. Such modifications may be to the point of nonobservance of a particular rule. For example, certain yards may practice the "blind" shoving of freight cars into an empty track, behavior to be discussed further in this chapter. One rule states, "Blind shoves must not be made on any track."

Often a particular accident on a division leads to an immediate superintendent's bulletin and then a permanent rule addition in the special timetable rules. On the Western Division of the CC & U, Engineer Jesse Krause ran past two restrictive wayside signs and through a 20 m.p.h. *shoofly,* or bypass track, at high speed with the crack *Transcontinental Limited.* An Urbana newspaper headlined "30 ARE INJURED IN [CC & U] DERAILMENT." As usual, the company issued a terse statement. "The derailment was caused by human error. The engineer overlooked a 20-mile-an-hour slow sign and a yellow caution signal entering the temporary track." Among the information printed by the newspaper was: "The engine units and two cars immediately behind stayed on the rails, but the next 15 twisted off at a small creek bed, jackknifing and banging along the walls of the ravine while passengers screamed and clung to hand-holds. Ambulance attendants worked for two hours removing the injured."

As a result, rule 16(u) was proclaimed, to increase the conductor's supervision of the engineer and to insure that air brakes are operative:

16(u). On train equipped with communicating signal, when a train order is received indicating that normal main track is out of service, and that trains are to be detoured through a siding, shoofly or other track requiring reduction in normal train speed, four sounds of communicating signal (Rule 16f) must be sounded [by conductor] two miles before reaching temporary track or route, and must be acknowledged by three short sounds of engine whistle (Rule 14h). Running test of brakes must be made as prescribed by Air Brake Rule 1029.

Rule 16(u) also prevents an engineer from claiming that the automatic air brake system was not operating well. Management often obviates alibis by such wording of rules and also "protects their own asses," as the men say.

In another incident, a flatcar ran away on the Paradise branch line and killed a person walking on the track further downgrade. This accident resulted in the insertion of a derailing switch into the branch line and in a special rule:

104(u). On Paradise branch, spring point derail is located in main track at M.P. 8.07, and must be locked in derailing position when not being used. Eastward trains and engines trail through derail. Westward [downgrade] trains and engines must stop and line derail.

RULES AS IDEAL AND ACTUAL PATTERNS

As a part of the formal organization of a railroad, the operating rules are sometimes ideal instead of actual patterns of behavior. The *ideal* concerns what people ought to or should do, whereas the *actual* concerns the behavior observable by an objective outsider (cf. Harris 1968:580). The focus of ethnological analysis here is not upon the achieving of or the backsliding from standards by personnel, but upon ranges of modal patterns of behavior (cf. Kluckhohn 1941; Deutscher 1966). Only a few examples need be given. Standard rule 34 requires that all crew members in a locomotive cab must communicate to one another the indication of each signal affecting their movement as soon as it becomes visible. *Ideally,* the men should call all block signals and all other wayside signals, including those indicating position of track switches (as shown by colored metal targets or lantern lenses) and various signs along the track. *Actually,* only block signals of restricting color are called, and green proceed block signals only when they are especially important—when starting a train or after a restrictive signal has been passed or is expected. Switch signals are not called unless the switch is lined the wrong way. The numerous kinds of wayside signs: 90-70, YARD LIMITS, W, DRAW BRIDGE, CENTRAL CITY ONE MILE, DERAIL, JUNCTION, BEGIN ABS, RESUME SPEED, A, and so forth are rarely ever called. It is impractical to call such signals, and even when a division officer is in the cab they are usually not called. Very rarely, depending upon the officer, all green block signals may be called.

Ideally, operating rules require that other crew members stop a locomotive if the engineer is not following the rules, for example, speed restrictions. Actually, few junior men feel able to intervene in the operating style of a senior engineer and, especially to reprimand him by using the emergency brake valve located in front of the seat of a fireman or head brakeman. (This valve is viewed by some as a kind of "panic button.") Further, the crew members on the opposite side of the cab from the engineer have no speedometer or air pressure gauges for the brake system and therefore are not able to make quick, informed judgments regarding use of the emergency brake valve. Is going too fast by 5 m.p.h. an emergency? What about 25 m.p.h., when the engineer is making a massive application of the brakes? Will we stop 50 feet in front of or 5 feet past the red A (absolute) signal? How can someone not operating the controls judge the point at which the head end of the train will stop? Few firemen or brakemen have ever attempted to second guess an engineer, who is in charge of a locomotive. The prestige, authority, experience, and informal social network among rails of the engineer as well as custom prevent the subordinate from "pulling the air" on a hoghead. Only some conductors (back in the caboose) can get away with such bold action.

Stone was faced with the above-mentioned dilemma once when firing on a fast freight streaking toward Crofts. He spotted and called ever more restrictive signals but noticed little reduction in speed on the part of the hoghead, who had twenty years seniority to his own one. When a single yellow appeared he bellowed, "YELLOOOWWW." The hoghead appeared to be going too fast to Stone, but he was not certain of the deceleration ratios of time and distance. The next signal was red and they overshot it by at least ten car lengths. The flagman from a local freight looked surprised as they ground to a halt some twenty car lengths from where his train had temporarily set out a few cars on the main line. About a quarter mile before the red signal, Stone could have pulled the lever on the emergency brake valve he was eyeing. But, by so doing, he would have stopped the train short of the signal and, possibly, derailed the train, throwing the conductor and rear brakeman about in the caboose. He would certainly have called adverse attention to the engineer and earned the man's enduring enmity. Instead, on the return trip with the second section of the livestock train, the hoghead, who had scarcely spoken to young Stone on the outbound run, chatted with him and entered into a temporary joking alliance with him to antagonize Jesse Krause. Such alliances were usually formed only among "old heads." Krause considered himself a fast runner and an air man. He was supposed to be fifteen minutes ahead of them with the first section of the livestock train and indeed Stone's second section never saw any trace of the first section; the signals were green all the way into Urbana Yard. However, in the locker room later, Stone's hoghead told Krause and all assembled that he and Stone had to be constantly on the lookout and reduce speed to avoid the restrictive block signals in the wake of the first section. Krause was miffed. On the round trip, Stone had been further enculturated into railroading: Do not pull the air on an old head, to whom one must relate for several decades on the job. So much for the rule that required him to "take action, when necessary, to insure the safety of the train."

A few operating rules are ritualistic, often meaningless survivals from the past. For example, according to the operating rules, most railroads carry green or white signal lamps on the front of certain locomotives (see Gamst 1975b:286). Green signals on a locomotive signify a following *section* of the same scheduled, regular, train. On the CC & U, and other railroads, "Extra trains must display two white lights by day and by night on the front of the engine." But, the glow cast by a pair of three-inch lenses of whitish or greenish glass cannot be seen more than a few feet from a locomotive in bright daylight, and thus the practice is functionless. (On some railroads, and on parts of the O & W, *all* trains run extra.) In the past, day signals were used—two flags of the color of the signal lights—but they have been discontinued on many railroads. Also, locomotives are dispatched on the CC & U from the engine house while displaying their train signals without authorization to do so and are run along miles of main line to their waiting cars, all before the particular train is authorized to come into existence. Oscillating white headlights are required to be used by rule under various conditions, but only some, older units have them. Why, then, does the rule continue, the men ask.

Some rules must be violated consistently to get work done in an expeditious manner. For example, when shoving long cuts (strings) of cars around curves, the engineer frequently loses sight, temporarily, of the switchman or brakeman who is guiding the movement. Trusting the man to jump off the side of a car and come into sight with a restrictive hand signal, the engineer continues shoving, temporarily "blind" in violation of the rules. Such action takes place under an unspoken pact between an experienced groundman and engineman. At other times, a true blind shove will be made, at a yardmaster's order, to save time and manpower. An engineer will shove a cut of 80 cars into a track of 120 car lengths with no one on the cars or along the track. Generally, the men feel that some degree of informed violation of some rules keeps the railroad operating more efficiently. In fact, exceedingly close and faithful observance of a few of the operating rules has been used by the men to "tie up" the CC & U. Cessation of the "religious" observance of the rules returns operations to normal. We should realize that rule violations of the kind discussed here are not the result of lack of or improper knowledge of a rule, or even of carelessness in observing it. What occurs is an informed "bending" of particular rules for certain purposes, but within the context of an overall knowledge of the rules and of their interrelations. In other words, violations of the kind just noted necessitate an understanding of the rules and the range

In mid-day sun, the main (lower) headlight on an extra train can be seen, but its two white classification lights on either side of the headlight do not give any discernible glow, even at this close range. See also photo on p. 91.

of variation of the consequences of their application or lack of application. Of course, railroad accidents do happen because of carelessness in using or lack of thorough knowledge of the rules.

EXAMINATIONS ON RULES

Two regular kinds of examinations and review on operating rules take place, the rules class and the efficiency test. The Chief Rules Examiner of the O & W system gives operating rules examinations and interprets rules to all operating officers and qualifies them as rules examiners so that they can instruct other employees.

The Rules Car   The rules examiner arrives in his special classroom car, a modified passenger coach, and holds the regular bi-annual rules examinations. Similarly, an air brake and mechanical rules examiner comes in his rules car to give his examinations and instruction. Examinations for initial employment and for promotion are written, oral, and, usually, practical. Bi-annual reexamination is usually oral. The rules examiner provides an informal horizontal link of communication between different subdivisions of the same and even a "foreign" railroad, whose crews operate over the tracks of his railroad. He relays operating and policy gossip and current events from terminal to terminal. At some isolated terminals in small towns, the visit of the rules examiner is a minor social event. His main function, of course, is to provide, reinforce, and test formal vertical communication between management and the workers. Rules examiners and some rails like to demonstrate their expertise with the rules, especially complex, arcane, or unfamiliar aspects of these.

Sometimes the examined show off their collective expertise to the examiner. In one instance, after asking several difficult questions on operating rules, which most of the rails in the rules car had difficulty in answering to his complete satisfaction, the examiner turned to block and interlocking signals which govern movement along and across tracks. The men were "laying in wait" for the expert and prepared a "rules trap" by asking questions on the supposedly immutable definitions in the book of rules. One rail asked the definition of a *home* signal.

"Simple . . . ," the expert replied, "a fixed signal at the entrance of a route or block to govern trains or engines entering and using that route or block." It followed, he said, that a home signal should be able to give a stop indication of some kind.

The rules man was then asked by another rail to give the types of fixed signals that could be a home signal. The examiner explained that *semaphore* signals (with arms or blades which give indications by their position) might or might not be home signals depending upon the color and shape of the end of the semaphore blades. However, *color light* signals (from which our highway traffic lights evolved) display their indications solely by lights of a prescribed color, and "all color light signals are home signals," capable of some kind of a red stop indication.

The rules trap had been baited by questions. Now it was sprung with a statement of local fact. Still another rail said, "Signal 9.8 on the Deepwater line is a color light which always displays a steady yellow. It never changes under any condition.

The rules examiner was befuddled. He ended the discussion by changing his stance from it could not be to it should not be, and he said he would report the problem to system management. Several years later he retired and nothing had ever transpired concerning the problem with the rules regarding fixed signals. As part of their reaction against the restraints of the system of rules upon their behavior, the rails on the CC & U delighted in recounting the springing of the rules trap. Collectively, the men had exposed a flaw in the company's operating rules and in the knowledge of its rules examiner, both of which they alleged to be imperfect.

As one conductor said, "The rules aren't airtight and the rules examiner sure as hell doesn't know everything about the rules." However, we should note that a rules examiner, backed by a railroad's rules committee, interprets and defines the rules for all.

A number of rails like to ridicule rules experts with railroad humor. This humor often has a didactic component. For example, among many standard definitions in the rules is the one of a railroad yard which begins with "a system of tracks . . ." and goes on for several lines. Road men parody the definition with a "practical" one of a yard, as they perceive it: "A system of rust surrounded by a fence inhabited by dumb natives lead by an idiot [the yardmaster] who will not let trains in or out." Their definition of a fixed signal is, "One that has been repaired."

Some of the rules instruction is informal by anecdote and outside of that intended by management. Once when Stone was attending a rules class, an examiner discussed the use of the locomotive bell as a warning signal. (By rule the bell *must* be sounded while approaching and passing highway crossings. But, when the diesel engines are roaring deafeningly in 8th run and the train is moving at high speed, a bell signal gives no discernible warning at a crossing.) When working as a locomotive engineer, the rules examiner had hit an auto at a highway crossing even though the flashing red warning lights were operating at the crossing, his crossing whistle signal was loud and long, and his headlight was on bright. As is customary, he had not turned on his bell. However, when he had stopped his train after the accident, he turned on his bell and let it toll incessantly the entire time that the police investigated the accident. He told the men in his class to follow his example and, "No one will ever accuse you of not obeying the rules by not having your bell on before a grade crossing accident." Stone made a mental note and was therefore further enculturated into the rule concerning the bell.

Pulling a Test   Efficiency, or practical, tests of operating rules have long been a part of railroading that is resented by the men. Reported in the *Railroad Gazette* (Anon. 1903:447) is an early example:

> The engineers protest against the false signal tests, which they say put them into jeopardy. . . . They say that James McCreagh [an engineer with 27 years service, who] had only been on the "Brown list"—the system of rewards and punishments—30 days in all that time, was discharged for overrunning a red switch target, when he was running 70 miles an hour . . . although he stopped so quick that he jolted his passengers up pretty hard.

Today, the CC & U/O & W gives numerous "signal tests." A frequent test is the red *fusee* (a railroad signal flare) for which, among other requirements, a stop must be made before any part of the train passes the signal. Engineers say that it is sometimes impossible to stop a heavy freight train going 70 m.p.h., against a succession of green block signals, before passing the fusee, given the distance in which it can be seen upon the roadbed. The years go by but the operating difficulties often remain the same.

Division officers try not to "pull tests" on fast time-freights that must be rapidly moved "over the road." A list is kept of engineers tested and not tested. The attention of an officer is focused upon engineers without recent tests, provided the particular run they are on at the time is not a "hot train." Safety tests with expediency is the underlying informal rule. When an official hides himself alongside the tracks to give an efficiency test the men call it "laying in the weeds." One former division officer, in discussing efficiency tests, explained to some rails that, "They'll lay in the weeds for you." He then related how a trainmaster told him, half in jest, "I'm going to get a hoghead on an efficiency test."

At times efficiency tests are meted out as a form of discipline. One engineer had a dispute with some divisional officers. Soon thereafter he was running on a short, double-tracked branch line with a STOP sign governing passage across an infrequently used spur of a foreign railroad which bisected the branch. As is customary, the engineer maintained the prescribed 15 m.p.h. speed for the branch, slowed before the spur, observed that nothing was on the foreign track and clunked over the railroad crossing. Two officials were waiting out of sight, observed his actions, and held an investigation which led to his being fired for many months.

Some men express hostility toward a carrier in recounting an event in railroading to other rails. The incident need not be entirely factual as recounted for this purpose because the manifest function of the tale is the venting of tensions and not the representation of experience. For example, John Grimshaw said regarding an efficiency test that he saw a red fusee from a great distance. Suspecting it to be a test by an official, he braked to a halt far from the fusee and "crawled" toward it. Such tests, he implied, could only delay the company's trains. "Let them pull as many tests on me as they want to," he concluded.

Generally, efficiency tests are not as frequent today as in the recent past. However, an automated efficiency test is present all along the line. Absolute block signals when displaying red (unlike other block signals) by rule allow no movement past them. Such signals record on a graph with a mechanical pen any movement past them when a red indication is displayed. "Getting by a red [absolute] one" is a major cause of being fired by division level officers.

Operating officers of a railroad division without question are exceedingly hard working and have great responsibilities. Road foremen of engines, trainmasters, terminal superintendents, and the division and assistant division superintendent are salaried employees who receive no overtime wages; therefore, they can be used sixteen or more hours per day, seven days a week at no increased cost to a carrier. Derailments, special trains with exacting movement requirements, and other constantly changing operating problems necessitate that these officers be on duty for very long stretches of time. Middle managers in other industries have nothing close to the broad obligations of these men who keep the trains moving and the cars delivered, no matter what the difficulty confronting them. Junior officers make less than the better paid of the men whom they supervise. Accordingly, many carriers find it difficult to keep anyone in some of the junior positions at some terminals. The operating officers who are responsible for getting the trains over the road on time are also responsible for enforcement of and supervision of use of operating and safety rules. The potential conflict of interest that exists in such a situation is sometimes realized.

Stone almost got by a red one in his first year. Engineer Lyme was letting him run a switch locomotive to get some experience. They were pulling 100 empty cars from a foreign yard up over a grade on a branch line, past an *interlocking* signal tower protecting the main line of still another railroad, and then downgrade after a junction with the CC & U main line into the Urbana Yard. The signal bridge spanning the three tracks at the entrance to the vast yard displayed three sets of red over red over red—all absolute signals. Stone did not realize that most of his cars were over the crest of the grade as he kept his train stretched with a moderate throttle, kept his independent (locomotive) brakes released, and, using his automatic brake valve, made a reduction in his train line pressure, braking his train to a halt a prudent six car lengths upgrade from the signal bridge.

When stopped, Stone applied the locomotive brakes (the throttle was already closed) and then released his automatic brakes along the train by increasing the brake pipe pressure to the standard 90 p.s.i. As the train brakes released, the slack in the stretched cars began to run in against the engine, which was shoved forward slowly while its brakes squealed against the great weight pushing downgrade from behind. In a manner of speaking, Stone appeared to be failing the automatic efficiency test of the absolute red block signal.

Lyme stormed, "Goddamn it! Don't you *ever* brake downhill with a stretched train against a red one!!" Stone frantically pulled his automatic brake valve lever over from running position (release and recharge) to service (reduction of air pressure and application of brakes). The releasing brakes slowly began to "set up" again and the automatic brake system caused the independent engine brakes to build up an excessive brake cylinder pressure. This pressure further retarded the snail's pace toward the three vertical red demon eyes. Out of pride, Stone did not "plug it," pull the automatic brake valve into emergency position. He allowed the independent pressure to build up perilously high. But he bled off just enough air to keep the locomotive wheels from sliding and thus making flat spots. He didn't want to "flatten the engine" and get by a red one all at once. He was able to get stopped a few inches from the absolute signal, which thereupon changed to a permissive indication. It took Stone five minutes to pump enough compressed air to recharge the automatic brake system and release the brakes on each car. By then, the signal was red again. Lyme expressed his heartfelt disappointment with Stone's performance.

I have introduced the reader to several kinds of railroad signals and this is a good place to review all of them in a systematic way. Railroad signals explained in a book of rules and always included in the questions of a rules examiner cover a wide number of kinds, several of which have many varieties. Generally, safe and efficient railroading depends on many interrelated signal systems. In these, symbols of different kinds communicate information, at times quite complex in nature. Among the signal systems are overlapping *hand, lantern,* and *flag* signals in which these devices are used to trace combinations of points, arcs, and straight lines in the air to transmit innumerable pieces of information. The rule books call all of these "hand signals," but the men, and often formal printed instruction of a carrier, call these "signs" in opposition to all other railroad signals. If a yard conductor working at night wants his locomotive with cars to back out of track eight, he gives an arc (five) and three points with his lantern (for a total of eight) and then a large circle (back up). When the engine has gone far enough, the conductor gives several, large, overhead arcs (slow/easy), each slower in proportion to the speed he desires. When his locomotive has pulled its last car past the track switch governing the track it must enter, the conductor gives a large, slow, lower arc with his lantern (stop, nonemergency). When the switch is thrown for the proper route, he motions the locomotive ahead with a moderately fast vertical motion of the lantern.

Locomotive whistle and *communicating* (air whistle inside of locomotive cab) *signals* use many combinations of long and short whistles. The *locomotive bell* and explosive, rail-mounted caps known as *torpedoes* each give only one signal. Verbal signals are invariably in the terse argot and technical terminology of rails. *Fusees* are flares; they are the technically most primitive of the colored light signals, an open flame. *Train signals* are colored lights, flags, or reflectors on engines and on the rear of trains. *Cab signals* are colored or positioned lights in the locomotive cab governing movement of a train and used in conjunction with fixed block or interlocking signals. *Fixed signals* are the largest and most diverse class of railway signals. These include: switch-attached colored lights, reflector lenses, and colored metal targets, indicating the position of a track switch; *train order* colored lights, with or without targets or semaphore arms, indicating any need to slow or to stop for taking delivery of written train orders governing progress of the train; *block* and *interlocking signals* using colored lights, semaphore arms, positions of lights, or combination of these to time-space and to control the speed of rail traffic in following and opposing movements along blocks (sections of track), or to control movement at crossings and junctions of two or more tracks with signals interlocked to prevent colliding movements; and *"boards,"* colored, lettered, and numbered signs used to control traffic, for example "STOP," "YARD LIMIT," "JUNCTION," "DRAWBRIDGE," "RAILROAD CROSSING," and so forth. (For further information on block signals see the highly informative "All About Signals" by John Armstrong—1957.)

RULES, A RETROSPECTION

The carriers usually charge "man failure" in a railroad accident. Actual man failure is sometimes engendered by the carrier's rules. The standard code contains all-important rule 99, the flagging rule, which invariably instructs a flagman (any train crew member) to "go back immediately with flagman's signals a sufficient distance to insure full protection." "Sufficient" is a subjective and ambiguous word as are other words used in rule 99, on the CC & U and other railroads. Thus, rear end and, at times, head end protection is provided for a train by means of a rule put into action by men having a varying range of subjective interpretations of the ideal and actual components of the rule. Authority, responsibility, procedures, timing, and sequences are unclear in rule 99 as in many other rules (cf. Devoe and Story 1973).

Interestingly, the earliest books of rules did not allow for any ambiguity with regard to flagging. In an era of low-speed operations, the 1839 rules of the Liverpool and Manchester said the following with regard to a *work train,* which builds or maintains track and structures along the right of way (Whishaw 1842:215):

> The Directors hereby give notice that when any ballast-train shall stop on the main-line. . . , the engineman shall send the fireman or one of the ballast-men four hundred yards back, with a signal flag, to stop any coming train, and the man shall remain on the look-out, till the ballast-train is ready to move.

Lack of respect for inexact rules leads to employee derision of certain of these. Regarding rule 99, a familiar rail joke runs as follows. A rear brakeman was asked why two of his fingers were heavily bandaged. He replied that the engineer had stopped his freight train and "whistled out the flag." The brakie went back a "sufficient distance" and laid down a pair of torpedoes (rail-mounted explosive caps for audible signaling). Just then the hoghead backed up to bunch the slack in the train, causing the caboose to roll back a few feet, and ran over the brakie's fingers. Such close-to-the-caboose flagging is called "drawbar flagging" because the flagman never leaves the *drawbar*, or steel shank, of the rear coupler of the caboose.

Conscientious flagmen, often students, are sometimes "left behind" when the train departs soon after recalling the flagman by one of several whistle signals appropriate to the circumstances. Once when a conductor was standing close to the drawbar of his caboose east of Cementon on a freight, the train began to depart. He shouted to his rear man, "Don't leave me!" whereupon the young rear brakeman, instead of pulling the air or signaling the engine crew, jumped off the rear platform of the caboose and joined his conductor in watching the caboose vanish over the horizon.

Sometimes the rear end crew is not left behind by accident. Quite recently, at Reed, a freight hoghead was angered ("fit to be tied") when his rear end crew led him back with a cut of cars into a very "rough joint" (heavy crash of a coupling) against other cars. The hoghead was bashed about in the cab. When the train was coupled and the air pumped up, he "took off," leaving the rear end crew standing on the ground.

It should be noted at this point that the standard rules which have evolved over a century and one-half of railroading are vital to safe and efficient operations and protection of life and property. The CC & U/O & W in particular have one of the better written versions of the standard code. (The most recent book of rules of the O & W system is issued under the signature of J. L. "Jimmie" Wolf, Vice President of Operations of the carrier and a former switchman at Urbana Yard. Wolf is regarded with fondness by CC & U rails as a local boy who made it to the top.) Virtually every standard or local operating rule was written for a compelling reason, often resulting from an accident.

For every railroader, effective, and hence "good," railroading is a balance between cautious obedience to the operating rules and sometimes taking informed chances by bending and breaking them. The "General Notice" before the general rules at the beginning of a book of rules says, "To enter or remain in the service is an assurance of willingness to obey the rules." The Notice also states, "Obedience to the rules is essential to safety." Unfortunately in the real world, safety and expeditious movement of railroad traffic are not always compatible. In many ways, the trade off between observing the rules and keeping the trains moving compels the railroader to do his flagging at the drawbar.

Those readers desiring more information on railroad operating rules should study an authoritative source on the subject, for example, Peter Josserand's *Rights of Trains* (1957), reprinted in paperback format. See also the AAR's *The*

Standard Code of Operating Rules (1965). Works of interest for the development of operating rules include Harry Dalby's *Train Rules and Train Dispatching* (1904), Harry Forman's *Rights of Trains on Single Track* (1904), and Warren Jacob's "Early Rules and the Standard Code" (1939). Recent works on particular aspects of the rules include NTSB 1971b on rules and accidents and Devoe and Story 1973 on the writing of rules. *Notes on Railroad Accidents* by Charles Francis Adams, Jr. (1879b) is a classic containing much valuable information on the rules and accidents as does the recent scholarly study by Robert Shaw, *A History of Railroad Accidents* (1978). The "grandfather" of all works on the code of operating rules is the American Railway Association's *Proceedings of the General Time Convention . . .* (1893). The Convention developed standard time for North America, originated the present standard code of operating rules, and is the predecessor of the American Association of Railroads. Its *Proceedings* are especially valuable for understanding the development of the rules because the discussions of formulation are included with the first codified version of each rule.

5/Freight train, freight train, goes so slow

In this chapter and the one that follows, we examine the central work and concern of the hoghead and other rails—train handling in accordance with the rules—by reporting on information from customary ethnological participant observation; we thereby take part in a typical run. But we also touch upon a number of other runs and incidents from on the job in order to broaden our understanding of the range of variation of behaviors and experience on a freight trip in American railroading. The quality of results from, intensity of data gathering in, and duration of the participant observation upon which these two chapters are based differ little from my participant observation among the Qemant peasantry of Ethiopia (Gamst 1969). Both examples of ethnological fieldwork produced results of research with a similar depth and richness of data. The second section of this chapter is presented not just to demonstrate conversational styles and interests of rails, but also to depict the extent of the governmental regulation underlying railroad rules and the operations guided by these.

THE CALL IS OUT

Harry "Slim" Rogers, a hoghead with over thirty years seniority, was sleeping the sleep of the dead when a constant pounding on the door of his room brought him slowly back to the world of the living. The call boy opened the door and flipped on the light switch, which caused a light blub to blind Slim temporarily. He heard the call boy saying, "Have you got that? And here is your call slip."

The door closed and Slim awakened further in the bed of a small single room in the company lodging building. Slowly, the words on the call slip came into focus for Slim:

CROFTS, MAY 27

Call UMX 26 [Urbana Mineral, originating on the 26th] OD 10 50 A
[On Duty 10:50 AM]
CONDR   E.S. SUMMERS
[Brake-   R.D. SPENCER
men]   T.F. HODGES

A clean Rock Island caboose awaits the arrival of a train so that it can be exchanged for the one on the inbound freight.

UNITS 2106 GR 7894 GR 1004 8805 2722
[Five different classes of units, two of which came from the Granger Railroad]
ENGR   H.R. ROGERS
OUT WITH 65 [loads] 18 [empties] 7038 [trailing tons]
S/O [set out] 10 350 AT GROVETON
CALL OUT 930A TTW [Initials of agent]

"They must have cleaned out the roundhouse at Central City," Slim mumbled to himself. "What a mix-match of units. This trip should be fun," he added ironically.

The hoghead showered, shaved, and dressed quickly. Before vacating his room, he raised the black shade over the window, turned off the light, and walked with his grip in hand over to the company "beanery" for some coffee and two sandwiches—one for now and one for later, on the road. Brother Rogers did not feel that he could eat one of the heavy breakfasts being served in the rectangular-shaped restaurant which was filled with the aromas of cooking bacon, eggs, hash browns, and hot cakes. "Brother" is a term of address and reference sometimes used by fellow members of a railroad brotherhood, or trade union, such as the Brotherhood of Locomotive Engineers.

BEAN TIME CONVERSATION

Chatting in the beanery with crew members of other trains, Slim said that he had not expected to be called until after the noon hour. The dispatcher had called a "close connection" on the UMX and wanted it run out of Crofts just as soon as it arrived. "They need all that power [units] at Urbana," cracked Slim's Conductor, Eddie Summers, who pulled up a chair and sat down next to Slim with a full breakfast. All of the rails present had "gone to beans," as, in their argot, they called mealtime.

Bob Spencer and Teddy Hodges, the head and rear brakemen, sat at an adjacent table eating with another of Rogers' brothers, hoghead Spence Gibbons. They all joined in the rambling conversations. It was 10:00 A.M. and they did not have to register on duty until 10:50 A.M. The three groundmen were well rested, being regular men in the freight pool from Urbana to Crofts. Slim was an extra board man and had been working with short rest for many days. He had hoped to catch up with considerably more than eight hours sleep in the company lodging house, when he arrived at Crofts at 1:15 A.M. the night before on an eleven hour, drag-freight run from Urbana. But now the shower had refreshed him and the coffee and conversation had awakened him fully—except for his stomach, which still felt leaden and mildly upset from sleeping odd hours.

It has always been the practice of the CC & U to provide inexpensive (twenty-five to fifty cents per day) or free lodging in private, spartan rooms for its road crews. The company's dormitory buildings at all of the away-from-home terminals are substantial, handsome edifices containing large army-style shower and toilet rooms, a good restaurant, and one or more lounges where men can converse, read, and play cards. The railroad station agent has an office in the building where he handles the company's business for his large terminal-station complex and supervises the calling of crews and trains on behalf of the train dispatcher. CC & U practice of providing lodging at nominal or no cost is an important safety factor on that property. Such practice virtually guarantees that its men will be sufficiently rested when departing from away-from-home terminals.

Rails who are not fully rested make more errors than those with adequate sleep. Those not fully rested rarely fall fast asleep on the job, but are involuntarily subject to what is known as minisleep, especially at night and during a routine, monotonous segment of a run, as on a steep mountain grade while at slow speed. During an attack of minisleep, the eyes close "automatically" and a man loses consciousness for a few seconds or minutes and then awakens abruptly. Slim Rogers had had a bout with minisleep on the run into Crofts the night before. His eyes had closed—for how long he was not certain—and then they opened. His heart was pounding. "Damn, I must have dozed. What was the color of signal 144.9? Should I reduce speed? Ah, there's the next signal and it's clear. I better stand up and stretch a bit." His heart slowed down to a normal pace.

The federal Hours of Service Act of 1906 fixed the maximum time on duty for operating railroaders at sixteen hours. (Hence, rails called it the "sixteen hour law.") In 1971 the hours of service were reduced to twelve. Such a reduction limits carrier flexibility in the assignment and handling of its crews, but also reduces fatigue among crew members, regardless of the amount of rest they have received. It was said that if one repeatedly worked sixteen-hour road trips or two consecutive eight-hour yard assignments it would "make you an old man before your time."

Slim and his fellow crew members tanked up on coffee in the beanery, and conversation turned to wayside signals. A "beanery queen" (attractive waitress, below the age of 70) filled all the cups again, as Slim related what he had learned at a recent meeting between officers of the Brotherhood of Locomotive Engineers (BLE) and two officers of the Federal Railroad Administration (FRA). Slim referred to the two FRA men in turn as the "senior man," who was a high level administrator, and the "signal man," who was a technical specialist on wayside block and interlocking signals.

The senior FRA man gave the obligatory praise to the assembled national, regional, and local BLE officers: It is as a "result of your support that we have a safety bureau at all." The brother opposite Slim at the conference table yawned slightly. The conference turned to the subject of false clear (green) and other false signals. Discussed was a recent wreck, on a railroad other than the CC & U, in which a freight train moving at speed along a main line headed in to a passing track occupied by a standing freight train. The track switches and block signals were under remote control. Crew members were killed and rolling stock and track destroyed. The FRA signal man said the accident was caused by the "man failure" of a railroad signal maintainer. The maintainer, he said, had done incorrect work on the home signal governing the junction of the passing track with the main line, thus causing a false clear (green) indication on the home signal. This signal was actually governing a 15 m.p.h. movement into an occupied auxiliary track, rather than a high-speed movement on an unoccupied main line, as indicated by the (false) clear.

A national BLE officer said he had talked to a national officer of the signalmen's brotherhood regarding the wreck. The signalman told him that man failure could not be the reason because the circuits for the block signals are checked constantly and thus incorrect wiring would be detected. Perhaps it *was* detected—by the hoghead who acted unwittingly upon the false clear, said a regional BLE officer sitting at the end of the conference table. The BLE officers agreed among themselves that the problem was in part one of a sort of jurisdictional dispute between "brother" rail unions over determining fault for an accident. Did a signal maintainer fail at his job, or did a locomotive engineer pass a very restrictive red over lunar white "heading in" block signal at high speed as if he had a "clear" to proceed down the main line?

Back at his table in the company beanery, Slim Rogers shuddered a bit thinking of the possible consequences of a false clear for a train running at speed. All rails present gave full attention to his account of the conference on false clears. A student brakeman sitting at the edge of the group looked somewhat shaken. "Has there ever been a false clear around here?" he asked.

He was told of one CC & U hoghead coming around a curve on a clear block signal and running into a self-propelled rail-coach for inspection of tracks. The car had not activated the circuits for the block signals, as it was designed to do. Consequently, he had a false clear. Recently, one night, a CC & U caboose and several box cars were sitting on a railroad crossing of a CC & U branch and the main line of a foreign railroad. The caboose was in a necessary "dead section" of the track circuit of the crossing and thus not detectable by the interlocking signal system. It was hit by a freight train proceeding at speed on a false yellow signal, which had thus not been warned of the crew car in its path. The hoghead of the foreign road was doing 45 m.p.h. against two successive yellow signals, when his headlight reflected off the CC & U caboose standing across his track about one-quarter mile ahead. He immediately pulled his automatic brake valve lever into emergency position, an act which also terminates all power to the traction motors geared to the axles of a locomotive. Nevertheless, his speed was still 40 m.p.h. when he hit the caboose with several thousand tons of freight train, which then derailed and plowed through the track structure for several hundred feet. The CC & U conductor working at his caboose was killed. The student brakeman now looked ashen. He had learned that while on the road the wayside signal systems are not always to be trusted.

Sipping his coffee, a veteran brakeman who had once worked for the Granger Railroad said that at Granger City a signal maintainer wired connections for green and red in reverse of one another on an interlocking signal. This defect was detected and no accident resulted. The Granger road corrected the defect and no one outside of local company management was the wiser. Too bad the FRA signal inspectors did not catch that one, the veteran brakie concluded.

Slim Rogers said a similar statement of regret had been made at the BLE–FRA conference. In answer the senior FRA man had said that there were only 260 inspectors in the FRA's safety department for all of the United States. The FRA tries to concentrate its inspectors on roads with a high percentage of defects in equipment. However, he said, we cannot go too far in such concentration because "good roads" would consequently tend to "slip." He indicated that the CC & U/O & W was certainly a good road.

Slim added that the signal man of the FRA had remarked that their signal inspectors must notify a carrier of any inspections or tests of signal equipment. They cannot touch a carrier's signals, for reasons of safety, without a responsible signal representative of the carrier present. Local managers of a carrier can thus check over and repair anything that an FRA inspector expresses an interest in before he reaches the signal, the signal man said. The FRA man concluded with, "When I go out and just look without a carrier representative [being present], about all I can say is that someone didn't steal the signals."

Slim said the senior FRA man then countered the narrative of the signal man by saying an inspector needs a carrier representative present if he is to point out any signal defects. Also the inspector does not always know in advance what he intends to inspect next. How, then, could the carrier know what to prepare for his inspection? Slim's coworkers at beans decided that reality existed somewhere between the accounts of the FRA senior man and signal man. "The senior man was just protecting his job," a conductor said. "He couldn't own up to any problems with his own operation."

IN THE REGISTER ROOM

Slim and his fellow crew members ambled off to the register room, arriving there ten minutes early. Another crew was about to "leave town" for Jackson and a third crew was registering in after a run from Urbana. Men sat on the long wooden benches and leaned on the rectangular tables covered with gear and register books. On the wall was a large standard clock so they could accurately check and set their railroad watches and against the wall was a table containing three different bulletin books. Posters admonishing safety on the job and careful car handling were on the walls, clearly visible, yet unseen by the men.

Eddie Summers, the conductor, learned that the UMX was late. (They would not leave Crofts for Urbana until 11:55 A.M.) It was not often they were called too early for a train. Further, their number of loads and tonnage would be somewhat greater than indicated on the call sheet. The crew registered in at the time called on duty, 10:50 A.M., read the bulletins, and started the entries on their time slips, to be turned in at the end of a run by the conductor for the ground crew, and by the engineer for himself and any other engine crew members.

Carefully, Slim placed his time slip in a folder, which he put into his grip. He then made some entries in his personal time book. Both the slip and the entries in the book would be completed when he registered off duty at Urbana Yard. He would then register his mileage earned on a special form maintained by his local union representatives. No one was allowed to earn more than his fair, union-allocated share of the mileage generated by the company's rail traffic. Operating employees in road service are paid by the mile (as are over-the-road truck drivers). Being paid by the mile is an incentive for high productivity among the men and has been in the contracts of railroad labor since the nineteenth century. "Making up time" is a basic value of road service employees, in part because of this incentive. This book does not deal in any detail with the lengthy and highly complex subject of railroad labor contracts and laws. For further information on this subject, see Lazar 1953; Horowitz 1960; Richardson 1963; *Industrial and Labor Relations Review* 1971; Rehmus 1971; Risher 1971; TFRP 1973; Aaron, et al. 1977.

Engine- and ground-men work in four major classes of service of which through freight is only one. Within any one class of service several general rates of pay exist per each 100 miles run. For engineers these rates increase above basic minimums by nine cents in passenger service and eighteen cents in almost every other class of service for every 50,000 pound increase in the weight of the locomotive on the driving (traction) wheels. The principle is that the heavier the locomotive is the more work that is done and the greater the engineer's responsibility and productivity. (The rates of a locomotive fireman-helper, when one is present, generally range from about 12 to 18 percent less than his engineer.) In all, hundreds of rates of pay are listed for engineers and for any firemen still employed.

Some of the "hotshot" fast freights running the 160 or so miles from Crofts westbound over the mountain chain to Urbana Yard make good time, covering the distance in only a little more than five hours. Some trains take almost twelve hours, up against the limits of federal law for the hours of service for a man on duty. In a recent four-day test period that I examined during the course of research for this book, crews of the total of twenty-six westbound freights averaged 7.62 hours on duty, after a layover at Crofts which ranged from nine to seventeen hours.

LEAVING TOWN

The UMX was at last resting in the passing track parallel to the main line at Crofts, its heavy diesel units murmuring as they idled. Hot exhaust rising from the stacks on the roof of each unit caused the clear air to ripple against the sunlight. The train would not be "yarded," put in the Crofts yard for switching of its cars or servicing of its units. Slim was accompanied by the student brakeman, who was making one of his student trips with the crew of the UMX. The hoghead explained to the student, after they entered the cab of the 2106, the kinds of freight trains the company ran: heavy trains (like the UMX), trains of moderate tonnage to achieve high speed (like the *Piggybacker* and the *Trucker*), and "caboose hops." A hop is a locomotive with a caboose and no freight cars, which is used to transfer locomotives and crews from one end of an operating district where they are in surplus to the other end where they will be in demand for outbound trains.

Slim continued explaining that the company never runs very short or light through freight trains with only 10 to 20 or so cars and 1000 or so tons. This is true even if the cars are waiting to be forwarded to the next terminal, and even when a caboose hop is called for a trip to the same destination. System officers play a numbers game and make the statistical averages for their freight trains look good, thereby showing good management on their part. High average tonnages of through trains are not to be diluted by adding a few waiting cars to a hop. The shippers' cars can wait for the next connection, whenever it may be scheduled. During 1977 in the United States, the average through freight train had 67.2 freight cars totaling 2030 tons. The CC & U/O & W had significantly higher averages; thus, their managers showed the many "wooden axle" (a term of derision) carriers how to railroad.

The student was surprised when Slim told him that the average freight train in the United States moves at about 20 m.p.h., even though many have top authorized speeds of 70 and 60 m.p.h. and a few are allowed to go a breath-taking 79 m.p.h.—all on unrestricted track. The *Piggybacker* and *Trucker* at times have train orders for the passenger train speed of 79 m.p.h. on the track between Central City and Crofts. Today, because of its ratio of number of cars having operative brakes to tonnage, the UMX was restricted by train order to 50 m.p.h. At times, trains with such cars and tonnage have been restricted to 40 m.p.h.

What Slim Rogers did not tell the student is that the average freight car is an expensive piece of capital equipment, costing over $30,000 when new. It spends over 40 percent of its life empty and over 40 percent of all freight car miles are empty car miles. Only about 12 percent of its life is spent in trains on the road. Even a moderate, 10 percent improvement in the utilization of freight cars would release an enormous amount of badly needed investment capital to the nation's carriers, which are financially hard pressed. The 10 percent efficiency would add the equivalent of over 130,000 cars to the fleet of class 1 railroads, thereby releasing over $2.5 billion dollars in investment capital. However, such self-help may be beyond the managerial and technological capabilities of the average carrier. One way to make car use more efficient is by being able to locate readily any car. This can be done through use of the Automatic Car Identification System (ACI), which is discussed in Chapter 8.

THE MAN IN CHARGE

Authority on a train has always been an intricate problem of relations between the conductor and the engineer. Bob Spencer, the head brakeman, had the student sit in the empty fireman's seat in front of his own on the left-hand side of the cab of the 2106. He explained to the student that Slim was waiting for a "highball" (permission to depart) command over the radio from Eddie Summers, the conductor, who was in charge of the train. Eddie was back on the caboose, almost a mile behind their cab. The student said he thought that the engineer was in charge of the train, or at least shared equal authority with the conductor. Bob showed the student the relevant rules governing train and yard service, including the phrase, "the general direction and government of a train is vested in the conductor and all persons employed on the train must obey his instructions." However, the engineer is equally responsible with the conductor for safe and proper operations and the two "must consult" when there is "any doubt as to authority or safety of proceeding." What "must consult" means is ambiguous and leads to friction between the engineer and the conductor. The engineer is officially in command of the train only when the conductor is incapacitated. Both men must "know" that other employees in their crew are familiar with applicable rules of all kinds and perform their duties correctly, must instruct them on the job as necessary, and must report "indifference, inefficiency, or insubordination" to company officers. All employees, whether operating or otherwise, are responsible on a passenger train to the conductor who "must know" that they are "alert and attentive" and, somehow, also know that they are "qualified." Actually, a conductor makes few judgments concerning the alertness and attentiveness of employees other than trainmen and enginemen. This is especially so since 1971, when Amtrak assumed the operation of most intercity passenger trains in the United States. Nowadays a conductor does not even "see" a chaircar attendant smoking in his car, let alone reprimand him.

In all, the conductor is formally in command of a train, and conductor and engineer formally share responsibility for safe operations. This joint responsibility is found in rule books going back at least to the 1870s and undoubtedly came about because the conductor is unable to control train operations totally from his location outside the locomotive.

The formal hierarchical division of authority on a train, as on a ship or aircraft, allows fulfillment of the transportation mission; safety of the capital equipment, crew, freight, and passengers; and takes into account that the mobile work environment is removed from the managerial supervision normal in other industries. The difficulty on a train is that the hierarchical relation of conductor over engineer is not clearcut. A fundamental problem exists with the authority of the conductor in that he cannot observe most signals and other conditions affecting the movement of a train and he cannot monitor much of the performance of an engineer. Many conductors monitor the engineer to some extent, but this activity is not uniform or entirely possible. A conductor might "pull the air" on an engineer if he feels that the train might not stop before passing a point where a freight car is to be handled or where a superior train is to meet or pass them. Conductors have a simple brake valve on the caboose of a freight train and a gauge indicating the pressure in the brake system, but no speedometer. Similar equipment is found on a passenger train. A vast majority of engineers feel that most responsibility for movements over the road is necessarily on their shoulders because the conductor is not in a position to know what is happening and what might need to be done in quickly changing situations. This attitude of engineers does not absolve the conductor from blame during investigations of accidents occurring on the road. The interpersonal conflicts between engineers and conductors fostered by the requirements of formal operating rules and the realities of operations are expressed in many ways and the tales that result from the expressions are legion.

Formal authority is the right to control behavior of others from a recognized social position. On a train it is not only clouded by the reality of operations but by informal privilege. This last is a right to behave in a particular way because of social characteristics other than authority. These could be a brakeman's skill as a car handler, an engineer's skill as an air man and fast runner, or a conductor's skill in manipulating the social system of railroading and countering some of the demands of management. Ties of kinship, friendship, and age-bonding are also important for privilege in railroading. Many rails are related by ties of blood and marriage, by relations built up over several decades on the job, and by the bonding derived from having been together during the same period of time as students and then as coworkers on varying rungs of the occupational ladder.

Privilege is manifested when an engineer gets to consult upon a conductor's plan of operations during the switching (handling) of cars or when the conductor, while temporarily on a locomotive, gets to sound the whistle or flash the headlight without asking the engineer. A senior brakeman or switchman might "play" with the locomotive controls, for example, surreptitiously opening the generator field switch so that power cannot be generated to start a train.

Authority itself may not always be directly asserted. A conductor in the yard might tell the engineer, "We're ready to go whenever you are." Instead of saying at the end of a meal period "Let's go back to work," a conductor might instead say, "Where did this short bean time disappear to?"

Exercise of authority and privilege results in numerous manifestations of social deference on the job. For example, a junior fireman, but not an engineer, might share his seat with a switchman during a movement over a main or branch line. Switchmen will leave vacant for a senior yard conductor a seat box often found on the deck of a locomotive cab for the use of switchmen. A senior man ("old head") may joke about a junior man's work attributes, appearance, or food without a counter jest by the person who is the butt of the comment. Most important, those without much authority or privilege, especially junior men, are usually addressed with very terse replies or commands in the line of duty, but are not generally talked to in a socializing way. In 1957 when Stone fired a steam locomotive on a branch line for an old hoghead, the engineer said nothing to him on the entire trip, except to acknowledge verbal signals. Going up a slight grade with all the cars the old hog could haul, Stone proudly "kept 'er hot." The needle of the steam pressure gauge was "on the peg," of maximum boiler pressure. The hoghead, afraid that the boiler safety valve would pop, bellowed, "Not too much steam!" Stone had his conversation for the entire ten-hour trip. Such are the wages of pride for a student. Students may listen quietly, but it is many years before they get to "old head it" with senior men.

After being given a "highball" over the radio, by the conductor, Slim Rogers released the locomotive brakes on his five diesel units and began stretching the slack in his train as he rolled toward the clear, dwarf signal governing his exit from the passing track at Crofts onto the main line to Urbana. The UMX was soon roaring down the line past West Crofts. Noticing that the next signal was clear, Slim began to study his railroad watch, the wayside telegraph poles, and the speedometer face of the speed recorder box mounted to his left. He was checking the accuracy of the speedometer. Like many railroads, the CC & U has 40 telegraph poles per mile with each mile marked by its mile post designation from the timetable. Up ahead a white rectangle bearing the black numerals 163 was attached to a pole (mile post 163 from Urbana). Glancing at the speed chart in his timetable, Slim figured that the one minute and eleven seconds that had elapsed while covering the measured mile meant he was actually going 50.7 m.p.h., even though the speedometer had read a steady 50. More than close enough, he thought. Some speedometers are faulty in their measurements to a considerable degree and this must be taken into account on a run. Many yard locomotives, also used in road service, have no speedometer at all, necessitating the use of a watch to check the speed.

Slim began to brake his stretched train as he saw restrictive block signals governing a junction some miles ahead. His initial braking at speed enabled him to assess the braking characteristics of his heavy train. Every freight train brakes differently and heavy ones have to be closely watched trains. The units thundered across a steel bridge spanning Dry River, filled with dust and rocks, as the train continued to decelerate with the force of the automatic air brake system. Every car in the train had its brake shoes squeezing against the treads of the car wheels. Slim kept the locomotive brakes released and prepared to reduce speed still further by easing off on his throttle. He had to be prepared to stop at the tower.

A few miles up ahead when he reached JN Tower, the hoghead received an absolute double red interlocking signal governing the junction with another line. This line was soon to be traversed by two sections of a westbound passenger train, No. 3, traveling some ten minutes apart. The pair were making up lost time on the transcontinental journey to Urbana. Running late, running fast, they would be doing 90 m.p.h. before entering the curve restricted to 80 m.p.h. some miles beyond JN Tower.

While the units of the UMX idled before the red signal, Bob Spencer related more of the conductor's role to the student, who could be promoted to that rank some day. Bob told the student that when operating over the track of another railroad, traversed by CC & U trains, the governing book of rules of that railroad gives the conductor the authority to take the locomotive of an inferior train if the one on his own train is disabled. He also told the student that operating rules of the traversed carrier have some interesting survivals from the days of the Old West, holdovers not found in CC & U rules. The "old time" rules include an admonition to conductors on passenger trains that, "Beggars, gamblers or unauthorized persons [includes prostitutes?] must not be allowed to practice their vocations on trains." Additionally, when "ejecting" a passenger from a train, because of an infraction of one of a wide variety of prohibited activities, "No more force than is absolutely necessary shall be used in expelling passengers from a train." The traversed carrier does not find it necessary to admonish the conductor further, as does the CC & U, that "in no case may a passenger be ejected except where shelter and food are available." Both carriers pass over stretches of landscape that resemble Mars.

While the student listened attentively, Slim and Bob chatted about the division of authority between conductor and engineer and, in so doing, recounted the time westbound No. 1, *The Transcon Flyer,* was lined down the wrong track at JN Tower. The timetable instructed, "Westward . . . trains entering JN Tower limits may move on clear train order signal in lieu of clearance card." A new towerman/telegraph operator was on duty at JN. He left the train order signal at the clear position on its mast, indicating he had no clearance card or orders from the dispatcher for the crew of the *Transcon.* However, he had the maze of switches, connecting five different tracks, lined up connecting the eastbound track from Urbana through the junction to the track diverging to Crofts. Instead of realigning the track switches by means of his controls in the tower, he allowed the line up to remain for an eastbound movement from Urbana to Crofts. The "student" towerman then gave a restricted speed interlocking signal to the *Transcon,* thus allowing it to enter the interlocking complex of tracks at slow speed. No. 1 then headed westbound onto the (left-hand) eastbound main line, which had no signals for westbound movements.

With no train order authority from the dispatcher to do so, the *Transcon's* engineer and veteran fireman (a promoted man for over ten years) were moving against the current of traffic on a 90 m.p.h. line. The crew would have no block signals to warn them of approaching trains because, as is normal on a double-track line, the tracks were not signaled for reverse movements. They prudently ran at a reduced speed, but, less prudently, had not consulted the applicable operating rules governing the novel situation. The timetable listed the district as having operating "rule 251 in effect." The rule reads: "On portions of the railroad designated in the timetable, trains will run with a current of traffic by block signals . . .". Rule D-151 provided the authority for the direction of the current of traffic: "Where two main tracks are in service, trains must keep to the right unless otherwise provided." According to rule D-R, a train order providing for a movement against the current of traffic should have been received by the conductor and the engineer of the *Transcon* reading:

NO 1 ENG 5090 WILL USE EASTBOUND TRACK AND HAS RIGHT OVER OPPOSING TRAINS FROM WEST CROSSOVER JN TOWER TO IN-TERLOCKED CROSSOVER EAST TOWER DRY RIVER

With such an order in effect, the rule book, among other things, instructs that opposing, eastbound, trains cannot leave the last named point until the designated train has arrived. All of the above would have been understood from a thorough reading of the relevant parts of the timetable and book of rules and could not have been learned from on-the-job experience. The experience of the crew of No. 1 at JN Tower was unique, as are so very many other operating incidents in railroading.

According to whichever account one finds more credible, the conductor either did not realize they were running on the eastbound line without the required written authorization, or he did not realize his crew was breaking the operating rules. The towerman realized his mistake and called Dry River, two stations down the line, telling them to hold any eastbound trains until the *Transcon* arrived. Meanwhile, the rear brakeman/flagman of the *Transcon* was busy throwing lighted red fusees from the rear of his moving train. Perhaps he thought the tower operator would line another train to follow them. When No. 1 arrived at Dry River, it was met by a delegation of company officers who inquired about the authority for the run from JN Tower. The crew was fired a short time later.

Discussion among trainmen and enginemen regarding the incident ranged from, *Does* the passenger conductor ever know what is happening? to, *Can* he know what is happening? The timetable instruction was changed to read: "At JN Tower, westward . . . trains may proceed with current of traffic on clear train order signal in lieu of clearance card." The next edition of the book of rules had a new rule following rule D-151 giving seven lines of regulations, not previously extant, on running against the current of traffic. Almost two pages of regulations were added by the carrier to the rules covering train order D-R. Now the men had more detailed written rules to consult when in doubt concerning reverse running. "Better late than never," remarked one hoghead regarding the additions to the rules.

THE DELAYER

Sitting in front of the red signals at JN Tower, Slim watched them remain red even after First and Second 3, the pair of passenger trains, had cleared the tower. The first section of No. 3 carried green signals on the front of its lead unit and gave a standard whistle signal of a long and two shorts, meaning that a second section was following, as authorized by clearance. Slim answered the long and two shorts with the acknowledging signal, two short blasts of his whistle. Second 3 also carried green signals and Slim again acknowledged. Soon a fast freight, Third 3, roared by at 70 m.p.h.—carrying green signals. For the third time, Slim acknowledged the long and two shorts sounded by an advance section of a regular (scheduled) train. Before the heavy and slow UMX, running as an extra (unscheduled) train authorized by train order, would be allowed to lumber out onto the main line past JN Tower, Fourth 3 would streak by, another fast freight—this time without green signals. However, Fourth 3 *could* have displayed green signals for a fifth section of No. 3, perhaps permitted by train order to run a number of hours behind its authorization by the timetable schedule of No. 3. If a Fifth 3 were authorized to run say three hours and twenty minutes late, Slim could run ahead of it without any fear of delaying it. He could run ahead of any regular passenger or freight train or section of a train just so he did not delay it by having it overtake him while he occupied a stretch of track that it was authorized to occupy by time-table or train order.

Before leaving JN Tower westbound for Urbana Yard, Slim and Bob reviewed the written "orders" with the student (who is nameless in this narrative, reflecting the rail view that a student's name is not significant). They had a *clearance card,* issued by a train dispatcher, which provides authority for a particular train or locomotive to move over a designated district. The clearance is addressed to the "C & E," conductor and engineer, and lists all *train orders* by their number. *Messages,* also having operating significance, are not listed on the clearance. An operating employee's timetable is used with the three kinds of paper authority for movements controlled by a dispatcher on his district.

In a distant office, the train dispatcher (often called "the delayer") is in communication with all manned stations along the lines he controls by means of telephone, telegraph, and microwave radio. He is also in touch with trains by radio, and by reports given to him by the *operators* manning particular stations. For example, as required by rule, Tom Jorgensen, the towerman/operator at JN, had given two sets of clearances and train orders to the crew

Page from an operating timetable. Scheduled meets and passes depicted in bold-face type. Multiple meets and passes are underlined. Instructions state that timetables of three other carriers must be used beyond West Bridge Jct. Any schedule may be annulled or run as two or more sections at different times. Numbers between station names are distances in miles and to the left are siding capacities in cars. Code letters are: f, flag stop; s, regular stop; TO, train order office; R, train-register station; B, superintendent's bulletin station; K, standard clock; I, interlocking; Y, turning track; P, dispatcher's telephone; D, diesel fuel; and T, turntable. Nontrain movements can occupy the main line in accordance with the rules in yard limits. All lines are single track unless labeled otherwise.

members of Slim's train. The dispatcher had previously authorized Jorgensen to issue the clearance and had dictated the train orders to him.

A dispatcher is the most important person in railroading. Most are men, but in the past few years a few women have entered this elite occupation and performed well as train dispatchers. These employees direct the movement of all trains, locomotives, and other self-propelled rolling stock (rail inspection cars, cranes) on the main and branch lines of a railroad district, often a division or subdivision. Through the efforts of himself and operators in way-side depots and towers, he coordinates the rail traffic by directing engine and train crews and maintenance-of-way personnel. Track and bridge repair crews must have their work coordinated with train movements so that disruption of traffic is minimized. Although long discussed by researchers (McCord 1948), only recently have comprehensive and systematic investigations of dispatching been made in the United States (Devoe 1974) and in the Soviet Union (Platonow 1971).

Dispatchers supervising CC & U trains control all of the six different kinds of railroad line. Unsignaled ("dark") main line and, commonly, unsignaled branch line, all with light traffic, are technologically the most primitive. Automatic block signals (ABS) are systems of color lights, semaphore arms, or other kinds of fixed wayside signals which govern the use of stretches (blocks) of track and which are actuated by a train or other rolling stock. Interlocking "plants" or stretches of track (as around JN Tower) have a system of signals, similar in appearance to those in the ABS, and of other devices, such as power operated track switches and derails that are so interconnected that their movements must be in an ordered sequence. Special interlocking operating rules are in effect on a stretch of track within interlocking limits. Such limits are often found at complex crossings and junctions of two or more railroad lines.

Centralized traffic control (CTC) is a technologic extension of an interlocking system, usually over a very long distance such as an entire division or subdivision. Its signals appear similar to those in ABS. The signals and many track switches, especially those for passing tracks and junctions, are controlled by the dispatcher who has a console panel before him. On the panel is a schematic diagram of the track controlled, including sidings, *crossover* tracks (from one parallel track to another), and most track switches, plus all wayside block signals—illuminated in color on the schematic. Locations of trains are shown by means of illumination of the affected part of the track diagram. Various control buttons and toggle switches on the CTC console panel enable the dispatcher to throw track switches and change indications of wayside signals by remote control so that he can arrange a clear route for a train or have it run into a siding and wait for another train. Dispatchers can be located many hundreds of miles from the district they control by means of CTC. The latest CTC consoles are entirely computer operated and are supervised rather than actually run by the CTC dispatcher, who can, however, override the computer. In all CTC operations, train movements are authorized by block signals, whose indications supercede other authority for train movement, such as timetable schedules. CTC adds to the capacity of a track to carry traffic, because it allows quick and flexible routing and spacing of trains. Single track with only ABS has a maximum capacity of about 30 trains per day and with CTC has a capacity of 45 trains per day.

ABS, interlocking, and CTC systems appear similar in their physical characteristics along a right of way. Their signals may be mounted high on a signal mast or on a signal bridge spanning several tracks, or they may be low ("dwarf") signals on ground level or slightly higher. ABS signals have a number plate showing location in miles and tenths of miles from a particular point; interlocking signals have no plate; absolute CTC signals either have a plate with the letter "A" or no plate; and the nonabsolute ones also have a number plate. Any of the three systems may be augmented by some version of an independent system of traffic control not involving wayside signals. Extant

A CTC dispatcher. His console has diagram of single and double track and sidings.

are various kinds of systems that could be lumped under the term "automatic train control" (ATC). These may or may not have cab signals with colored or other visual indications given within the locomotive cab and reflecting the same conditions as any of the other three systems just noted, but independently of them. All forms of ATC have audible signals in the cab, such as warning whistles. With ATC, train brakes are automatically applied and locomotive tractive power is cut off when the system senses a violation of operating rules regarding reaction by the engineer to a particular signal indication or, at times, other speed restriction.

A sixth kind of railroad traffic control is a manual block. In unsignaled territory, which would otherwise be "dark," a series of long blocks are created, often by use of the manually operated train order signal at a wayside depot, upon information sent by telegraph or telephone train orders. Dark and manual block districts are survivals from the earliest days of railroad operations in the early and mid-1800s.

On otherwise unrestricted track with the proper rolling stock, the speed limits for each kind of territory is generally as follows: dark, 49 m.p.h.; manual block, 65 m.p.h.; ABS, interlocking, and CTC, 79 m.p.h.; and supplemental ATC, 100+ m.p.h. With present-day technological capabilities, the ideal high-speed, high-density-of-traffic line should be one having CTC and some form of ATC. Helpful also on such a district would be the elimination of written train orders, clearances, messages, and timetable schedules in favor of an in-cab, computer-display console which could give and monitor all of the information needed by an engineer for efficient and safe operations. Monitoring would include an alertness testing device which would sense continued movement by the engineer. Such an electronic "console-conductor" might be the only way to solve effectively the problem of conductor-engineer authority on a train.

Slim Rogers had the throttle on the eighth notch and was accelerating from the 30 m.p.h. to which he had been restricted by the speed board reading "30

30" that governed passenger and freight movements from the Crofts line through the interlocking plant at JN Tower. The line around Crofts is CTC territory; west of the tower is ABS and ATC territory for many miles.

About five miles out of JN Tower, the UMX passed the siding at Hendricks. It was occupied by a westbound local freight, which had waited for the four sections of No. 3 and now for the UMX—running as Extra 2106 West. The local would follow the UMX as soon as the dwarf signal governing the exit from the passing track changed from red to yellow. Both the UMX and the local were extra trains, not authorized by a timetable schedule. As extra trains, each carried white signals on the front of their locomotives. In the signal color coding of the nineteenth century, white was a proceed-safety and green a caution signal (Gamst 1975b:279–292). Today's train signals are survivals from the past. The green of a preceding section warns of caution, and the white signifies safety to a train about to pull out onto a main line, although the original symbolism is lost on today's railroaders.

The dispatcher had given permission for the local to switch its cars for 30 minutes after the passage of the four regular trains and the extra, the UMX. He was running Extra 2106 West another 40 miles, to Cementon, where he would have it pick up several cars. On the telephone, he was already talking to the operator-agent at Cementon depot regarding the pick up of the cars, loaded with cement. "Have the UMX pull in the clear and pick up the loads on Johnson spur. And don't let them leave town if they are still on the time of No. 15! I don't want it to be delayed again on the hill by a mineral train." Far to the east, No. 15, a passenger train, was racing westbound toward JN Tower.

6/On the high iron

RUNNING TO CEMENTON

The stretched UMX rolled along the "high iron," the relatively tall and heavy steel rails, weighing over 130 pounds per yard, which make up the heavy main line track. The extra created the usual track-train dynamics of the passage of any train. Depending upon speed, condition of track, and kinds and conditions of rolling stock, as the train moves *forward* along the track, its units and cars also "hunt" *vertically* and sway *laterally*. Excessive lateral and vertical motion can cause "rough riding" of equipment. Certain classes of locomotives are recognized by the men as being especially rough riding. At certain low and moderate speeds, just the right oscillation of a train can cause the track to break apart or the cars to derail, especially if the track is in poor condition, a condition fortunately not existing on the route of the CC & U.

Suddenly, Slim began sounding the standard warning on his whistle. It was then that the student thought he could see some small, grayish shapes about a mile ahead on the track. "Gandy dancers," Slim called to Bob. As the UMX rolled by at 40 m.p.h. a section gang of maintenance-of-way, or section, men leaned on their tools and observed the passage of the train. The "Gandies" were giving the train a *roll by*. Their experienced eyes looked for hot axle bearings, sliding or broken wheels, sticking brakes, swinging car doors or other loose car parts, dragging equipment or lading, or shifted loads on open cars. The foreman of the section gang gave a highball signal with his hand to Teddy Hodges, the rear brakeman. All was well with the UMX. The towerman at JN had previously rolled them by as they passed through his interlocking plant. Immediately after the UMX passed them, the section gang went back to raising slightly the north rail and to "smoothing" the rail in the vicinity of a nearby track switch. They had been given a modest amount of time by the dispatcher until the next eastbound train was due at their worksite. They would complete their work without slowing a single train.

Just as a hunter among the Australian aborigines can see the signs of the passage of an animal where the unpracticed eye sees nothing, so too can experienced railroaders discern animals, people, and equipment far ahead on the track where the average person would see nothing. Slim's eyes had already picked out the color of the next block signal, which the student had not yet been able to resolve in the bright noon sun. "Double yellooww," Bob bellowed from across the cab, and Slim responded in kind. The hoghead's mind was partly occupied with the Dry River terminal, which was a few miles to the west.

A hoghead had to have his wits about him in order to bring in a heavy train through a conjested terminal area with its complex of intertwining tracks and its special operating rules which apply only in the particular terminal area. Slim reflected on the experience in the Dry River terminal that his old friend, Tom Potter, had recently related to him. Tom was one of the better hogheads on the CC & U. Coming into Dry River with a heavy train, Tom "set ten pounds or so" with his automatic brake valve and brought his speed down to 15 m.p.h. and then "kicked off the brakes" in the automatic system of the train. He was a prudent 5 m.p.h. under the maximum authorized speed for the block signal indications. Coming around a curve on his running track at the far end of the Dry River Yard, he saw on the ground up ahead a dwarf signal indicating absolute-red. Immediately, he made a second set of the automatic air brakes, but the system was not yet fully recharged. Tom allowed his locomotive brakes to build up their brake cylinder pressure. With the aid of the locomotive brakes, it appeared he would stop just short of the red eye gleaming up at him. As the locomotive brakes retarded his units to a speed slower than that of the trailing freight cars, "the slack ran in." It was the slack action of his heavy trailing cars that shoved him two car lengths past the absolute red. A mechanical pen recorded this transgression on the graph of an instrument in a nearby tower. Slim spoke to Tom the day before the company officers held their investigation of the violation of rule 271. Slim found Tom visibly agitated and nervous, perhaps because his friend had no record of such an incident in thirty years of engine service. Slim tried to console Tom, and then sympathized with him again when Tom was fired a few days later. The Brotherhood of Locomotive Engineers would eventually get management to return Tom to service.

The next signal was a single yellow and the next a red over yellow. Slim made a reduction in his brake pipe pressure of 8 p.s.i. in order to apply the brake under each car in his train. The roar of escaping compressed air filled the cab. It took about a minute for the braking impulse of the reducing brake pipe pressure to reach the caboose, where the rear-end crew observed the reduction on their air pressure gauge. After slowing the UMX, Slim released the brakes and now moved ahead at 30 m.p.h. He allowed his speed to drop further to 20 m.p.h. The hoghead began threading the heavy UMX through the approach tracks of Dry River Yard, a large terminal enroute to Urbana. The red over yellow was an authorization to proceed at restricted speed only: permitting stopping short of other rolling stock, obstruction, or track switch not properly lined, and not exceeding 20 m.p.h.

He might have to stop the ponderous UMX at any moment in half the distance seen to be clear (in case of another movement on the same track coming toward the UMX, which is permitted in yard limits). Entering the yards of the terminal area, he saw his next signal displaying an aspect of flashing yellow over lunar (a white color). Slim was now authorized to proceed at 30 m.p.h. over a diverging route lined up for him from an adjacent tower. However, he kept his speed down to just a little over 20 m.p.h. until he could see a more permissive signal indicating that more than one block of track up ahead was clear. "Clear," the student yelled from across the cab. He had called the signal governing another main track. Bob smiled and informed the student where their next dwarf signal would appear as they exited from the terminal complex. Back on the caboose, the rear-end crew could see none of the signals governing the complex of tracks in the yard area.

The dwarf signal was yellow, but the next was an unrestricting clear (green). Slim's stomach muscles relaxed and he began to stretch his train and accelerate. As the caboose came onto straight track, the 7348-ton train, pulled by five units totaling 15,900 h.p., began to surge ahead. The engines gave a deafening roar as they belched smoke and some sparks. Slim now had the throttle wide open, to the eighth notch. The UMX had 2.2 h.p. per trailing ton and 82 trailing tons per operative brake (one to each car). The hoghead had to keep these statistics in mind as he wheeled his 50-m.p.h. mineral train westward toward Cementon. Narrow canvas sun awnings above each of the two side windows of the cab flapped audibly in the breeze created by the motion of the UMX.

Slim looked at a message he had received from the operator at Dry River Tower: "C&E EXTRA 2106 WEST. CLEAR NO 15 ENG 6844 AND NO 25 ENG 50 . . . ON TIME." They would make it to Cementon well before they were "on the time" (schedule) of train No. 25, but 15 was going to make it a close call. This was especially so since Train Order No. 7 read: "ON BOTH TRACKS SPEED LIMIT 30 MPH BETWEEN 6 POLES EAST OF MP 110 AND 1 POLE EAST OF MP 110 BETWEEN BREEZE AND SIMS." A second message would affect them after their switching at Cementon: "C&E EXTRA 2106 WEST. CLEAR FIRST NO 53 1 HOUR LATE [behind timetable schedule] DRY RIVER TO CEMENTON. 40 MINUTES LATE CEMENTON TO APEX. 20 MINUTES LATE APEX TO PIEDMONT." Still a third message read, "PICK UP CEMENTON 6 LOADS FOR URBANA ON JOHNSON SPUR." Finally, one last train order affected them only to a limited extent. Train Order No. 9 read:

EXTRA 4439 WEST LEAVING DRY RIVER ABOUT ONE FIFTY 150 PM HAS 1 CAR OF EXCESS WIDTH. YOU ARE PROHIBITED FROM RIDING ON THIS CAR ACCOUNT INSUFFICIENT CLEARANCE. THIS TRAIN MUST NOT BE PASSED ON NEXT ADJACENT TRACK BY ANY TRAIN HAVING CARS OF WIDTH IN EXCESS OF 11 FEET OR OVERHANGING LOADS. NO MEETING OR PASSING PSGR DOME CARS ON CURVES M P 155.2 M P 155.5 M P 180.9 M P 181.2 AND M P 181.6.

Bob explained to the student that railroad typewriters for operations do not have lower case letters.

The hoghead consulted his timetable and made some calculations with a ballpoint pen on the face of one of the messages. If he kept his speed right on 50 m.p.h. as he raced across the flats to Cementon with his heavy train, he would clear No. 15 by about five to ten minutes, if the 90-m.p.h. passenger train were approximately on time. If No. 15 were exactly on time, the UMX might give it a few restrictive block signals back along the westbound main line. Eddie Summers called softly over the radio, "Let's go all the way [to Cementon], Slim." Now they would both share any blame for "stabbing the varnish" (delaying a passenger train). Anyway, Eddie would not "pull the air" (apply the brakes) on Slim.

Bob shrugged his shoulders and yelled across to Slim, "If we stab No. 15, the hoghead won't have to watch his timetable so closely to keep from getting ahead of schedule."

Slim was not so cavalier about the possible stabbing. Some of the blood let might be his own. The trainmaster at Piedmont had already warned him, twice, not to stab any more passenger trains with a slow, heavy mineral train. Slim had done a good job of stabbing recently with a coal train. Bob was correct that within non-CTC territory, a train could not leave a station ahead of its scheduled time shown at that station in the timetable. Also, a regular train running late could be operated with less strain upon its hoghead. All he had to do was observe the speed restrictions imposed by the gear ratios of the traction motors of his units, the ABS and ATC, the wayside speed boards, his train orders, and other requirements. Regular trains, such as Nos. 15, 25, and 53, unlike Extra 2106 West, were authorized by a timetable schedule in effect until the train was twelve hours behind schedule or annulled by train order.

A station, Bob explained to the student, is not necessarily a depot, tower, or other building. It is simply a place designated in the timetable by name. Up ahead was a passing track and on a post was a white, horizontal station sign reading "STONE CREEK" in bold black letters. That was all there was to that station listed in the timetable among the stations between Dry River and Cementon. The timetable listing also noted that the eastbound and westbound passing tracks at Stone Creek each had a capacity of 120 cars and a phone booth with a wire to the dispatcher. And the main line around the station was controlled by ABS and ATC.

Because of his maximum speed restriction, Slim did not have to slow for a half-dozen curves posted at 60 and 55 for freight trains. He did slow for a curve posted at "40 40." Even No. 15 will have to get down to 40 m.p.h. for that curve, Slim thought to himself. A headlight was up ahead on the westbound main line. Slim dimmed his headlight and the other hoghead dimmed his as well. It was an eastbound "drag" of 115 empty cars. The drag was also not going to get anywhere in a hurry. In fact, the drag, an Extra East, had a message to clear a fast, time-freight and to do so meant heading in at Stone Creek in order to be passed by the time-freight. The drag would just fit at Stone Creek; otherwise the hoghead and conductor would have headed into a previous passing track.

Accelerating to 53 m.p.h. after rounding the 40 m.p.h. curve at 45, Slim continued running over the rugged, semi-arid countryside, with its mixed sandy and rocky soil and coarse vegetation. The intense heat caused the air up ahead to ripple, distorting all visual images. Ahead in the brilliant sunlight a small track car had been pulled off the main line into the clear on a special turnout and the gandy dancers looked as if they had just finished getting off the high iron. Bob explained to the student that section men have not used hand-pumped track cars for many decades; instead, the cars are motorized with a small gasoline engine.

These small, easily man-handled cars are actually self-propelled, four-wheel platforms capable of hauling a few men and some equipment at slow speeds. They are constructed so that they will not actuate the wayside signal systems or the ATC and thus chance delaying a train. Instead, the section men receive permission from the dispatcher to occupy the main line during specified periods between the passage of trains. Occasionally, these little cars are hit by a train, sometimes killing or injuring the occupants. Special automobiles, equipped with an auxiliary set of flanged steel wheels for traveling on tracks and known as hy-rail cars, are used by carrier officers on their rounds of inspection. These cars can actuate the wayside signal systems and are consequently afforded protection against trains.

No. 15 was due out of Dry River at 1:25 P.M., would roar by Stone Creek at 1:46 and Ridgeway at 1:55. The passenger train would be by Cementon at 2:03, where it might make a flag stop to receive or discharge passengers or it might keep right on going. No. 15 would slow to 30 m.p.h. and its hoghead would see if the depot agent held out a white signal flag, thereby requiring a flag stop. If the conductor on No. 15 or the agent at Cementon did not signal for a flag stop, the hoghead would begin to widen on his throttle and leave the 30 m.p.h. restricted track of Cementon at speed.

Doing 55 m.p.h., Slim passed the one-mile-to-siding sign for Ridgeway. This was the point of no return; he could not possibly stop his stretched train in time for the track switch giving entry to the Ridgeway siding. At 56 m.p.h. he was going a mile every minute and two seconds according to the speed table in his timetable, which he had propped up on his controls. No. 15 was doing a mile every 40 seconds, Bob reminded him. The head man further noted it was now 1:45 and No. 15 was due past Stone Creek. They were exactly nine minutes ahead of the passenger train. No. 15 would eat up the five miles from Stone Creek to Golden and then the pair of five-mile stretches from Golden to Ridgeway and from Ridgeway to Cementon in no time at all—actually, in seventeen minutes according to the timetable. Could Slim decelerate the UMX and then crawl into the siding at Cementon, through the 15 m.p.h. turnout, in time to clear the main line for No. 15? A station sign flashed by on the right: RIDGEWAY. "We could always back into Ridgeway," said Bob, not at all helpfully. "Or else," he said, "we could get Teddy to bust a red fusee and drop it. That would sure cool off No. 15."

The student looked puzzled, so the head man remarked that they could have Teddy, the rear man, ignite and drop onto the track a red signal flare. The crew of No. 15 would be required by rule 11 to stop, extinguish the fusee, and then proceed at 20 m.p.h. for one mile before resuming their pace. Bob explained this was just part of the ribbing he was giving Slim, and that the student should not take seriously the suggested use of the fusee. Bob was merely relieving his own tensions by transferring them, in jest, to Slim. The student then reread rule 86 which stated, in part, "Within automatic block system limits an inferior train must clear the time of a superior train in the same direction only sufficiently to avoid delay to the superior train." Dry dust swirled in the roadbed as the UMX passed through the area of an exceptionally arid pan, the color of chalk. It was said that even a vulture had to carry a canteen of water at this time of year.

The hoghead had the UMX slowed down to 35 m.p.h. on a clear block as he passed the sign indicating one mile to Cementon passing track. He was already rolling through the hills covered with cement dust in the outskirts of the industrial town. Across to his left, an industrial switch locomotive of a noncommon-carrier short line was hauling a string of cars down out of the hills to the main line at Cementon. In four minutes the UMX would be "on the time of No. 15," thus violating rule 86. At 2:01 P.M. Slim stopped his train, through coordinated use of his dynamic brake and locomotive air brakes, only ten feet from the track switch on the main line into the east end of the siding. If he had used the automatic brakes on the entire train, it would have been a few precious minutes until they were pumped off and released— minutes they did not have. Bob was on the lowest of the steps on the right front of the 2106, and he hit the roadbed running before the train had ground along its final few feet to a halt.

Slim was already releasing his locomotive brakes and beginning to notch back on his throttle as Bob pounded the final few steps over the gravel at the edge of the wooden ties. The head man unlocked the large standard padlock on the switch stand with his brass key and pulled the steel handle of the switch stand up out of its main line notch and over into its siding notch. Quickly, he put the open hasp of the lock into the ring securing the handle. (Teddy would lock it when he realigned the switch for the main line and the passage of No. 15.)

Bob motioned the UMX ahead with his arm, but the 2106 was already inching toward the switch. It was now 2:02, and the passenger train was due past the Cementon depot, about one-half mile ahead to the west of them, at 2:03. By now No. 15, if on time, would have slowed for their double yellow block signal, slowed still further for their yellow, and then stopped and proceeded at 20 m.p.h. for their red signal. The passenger train might be in sight of the UMX's caboose, with its red marker lights indicating it was on the main line. Slim wondered if he should have sounded a long and three shorts on his whistle (i.e., flagman protect rear of train). However, he had stopped only a very few seconds and did not want to leave Teddy behind about a mile or more from the east track switch at Cementon.

Back on the caboose, Eddie Summers had peered off into the distance for the bright headlight of No. 15, but he could see only empty track. As the caboose of the UMX finally rolled into the clear of the main line at 2:05, Teddy threw the switch into the main line position and its red target moved from its aspect at a right angle to the track to one parallel to it. Thus the target was not visible to a train on the main line. The rear man snapped home the hasp of the lock after placing it in the ring staple of the switch stand; now no vandal or idle passer-by could throw the switch. Meanwhile, just as Slim had turned off his headlight, the conductor had extinguished the red *marker* lamps. Both men thereby signaled according to the rules that they were clear of the main line, at long last. Slim's muscles relaxed and he slouched in his seat, taking the tension off his strained back. Bob told the student what was being done with the markers on the rear end and reminded him that it was a marker, or markers, that officially designated a movement as a *train,* which, according to the rules is "a locomotive or locomotives coupled, with or without cars, displaying markers." Display of markers on a movement allows rails to know that it is a train running on timetable schedule, train order, or other authority.

No. 15 came by at 2:11 P.M., carrying no (green) signals, and made a flag stop for passengers. Bob learned from the station agent that the local freight the UMX had passed earlier had had a "dynamiter" in the cars it was switching on the main line, and the defective car had caused a delay to the passenger train. A dynamiter is a car with defective air brake equipment which causes the car to apply its brakes and those of the entire train in emergency application when only a lesser brake application is made by the engineer. It takes many minutes to pump off and release any emergency brake application.

PICKING UP CARS

After Bob uncoupled the units from the train, he rode along the running track on the front steps of the 2106 as Slim moved the diesels at 10 m.p.h. and then slowed to 2 m.p.h. at the switch stand to Johnson spur. From his position on the steps of the rear unit Teddy, the rear man, gave an "easy" (slow) sign with his arm and then dropped it in a "stop" sign. He threw the track switch and Bob and Slim saw the red metal target on the switch stand flash into position at right angles to the running track. In accordance with Teddy's hand signals, Slim backed the five units against the six covered *hopper cars,* loaded with cement, which they were to haul to Urbana. As typical hoppers, the cars had one or more compartments funneling to a covered opening or openings at the bottom. The coupling was made by snapping together under the pressure of the rolling stock the automatic couplers between the rear diesel unit and the lead car. The coupler is a heavy device for joining cars by means of interlocking, flexible steel jaws at the ends of spring-loaded steel shanks. Next, Teddy motioned Slim to move ahead slightly in order to test the couplings between the units and all six of the cars. The couplers were tightly locked.

After closing the angle cock valve on the air hose at the rear of the last hopper car, Teddy had the student couple the air hoses by hand between the rearmost diesel unit and the head hopper car. Compressed air hissed as each car's automatic brake system began to charge. Teddy instructed the student to release the hand brake on the head three cars by turning each hand brake wheel counterclockwise, to release position, thereby loosening the tension on the chain which applies the brake underneath the car. The hand brakes prevent the cars from rolling during the period in which their brake systems are not charged with air from a locomotive.

Teddy motioned Slim ahead. He and the student rode on the rear car and dropped off at the switch stand, after motioning Slim to slow and then to stop. Bob remained on the lead unit with Slim. Teddy guided the movement of the five units, shoving slowly the six loads back to the waiting train. He coupled the last hopper car to the lead boxcar of the train and tested the coupling by having Slim ease ahead. Next Teddy told the student to couple the air hoses and to open slowly the angle cocks between the rear hopper car and lead boxcar of the train. Opening the angle cocks too fast could cause the automatic air brake system to go into emergency application. It would then take Slim twenty minutes or so to recharge the brake system after such an application.

Eddie, the conductor, gave Slim a "set up" [the brakes] command over the radio. He then observed the application of the brakes on his caboose before giving Slim a "release" command, and observing the release. The crew now knew that the brake pipe and its functioning were again continuous from the lead diesel unit to the caboose. Bob and the student walked up to the 2106 to join Slim. Teddy waited until the caboose rolled by him instead of walking back to it. Eddie gave Slim a "highball" command from the caboose, and the train began to roll slowly down the running track toward the green dwarf signal governing the joining of the westbound main line.

RADIOING AHEAD

As the UMX rolled out onto the main line with Eddie and Teddy sitting up in the cupola of the caboose, the conductor called the dispatcher over the radio to let him know that they had picked up all of the cars. The UMX now had 74 loads and 22 empties for a total of 7977 trailing tons, averaging 83 tons per operative car brake. The units smoked visibly as they began to move uphill into the 1.6 percent westbound grade of Maxwell Pass, as the route over Maxwell Mountain was called. Eddie then said a few words over the radio to Slim about the message to clear No. 53, *The Overland Express* (40 minutes late) at Apex, the summit of Maxwell Mountain. By using the radio, Eddie could perhaps get more time on 53 from the dispatcher, if it were more than 40 minutes late out of Cementon.

Observing either side of their train from their seats in the cupola of the caboose, Eddie discussed the use of the radio with his rear brakeman. The advent of train radio meant that under certain conditions crews could call the dispatcher to see how much additional time they could "get" on the schedule of a superior train. However, oral instruction cannot supersede that of a train

Engineer radios yardmaster for permission to leave town.

order. At times, when listening on a yard radio or on a road radio, rails are informed of current events as they happen: A train is attacked by teenagers throwing stones at Monroe Junction; a derailment has taken place up ahead; a brakeman has been hurt releasing a balky hand brake; or an engineer is having trouble with one of his diesel units.

The microwave radio system now found on all railroads supplements, and virtually replaces, the older telegraph and telephone communication binding together a far-flung carrier. The two-way radios in cab, caboose, and way-station have one or more preset frequencies, or channels, designated for use by a particular carrier. CC & U units have a road and a yard channel for their own territory and several other channels set to the frequencies of the Granger Railroad and a few other carriers over which CC & U units customarily operate.

Generally, radio makes anticipation of conditions easier than in the days before its widespread use. Eddie and his rear man recalled that on a recent run they were following Second 15 with an extra freight train. They heard on the radio that a heavy train of cement was due to leave Cementon. Consequently, they kept on the double yellow block signal of second 15, in effect making themselves an unofficial third section, as far as the cement train was concerned. The cement train thus did not have enough time to get out on the main line in front of them.

When operating in fog on a grade, while following behind a train, the engineer can radio the train ahead for its running speed and thus keep from getting too close to it. This is especially important on upgrades with block signals bearing plates with the letter "G," since a hoghead does not have to stop for these grade signals when they are red. Also, some parts of the line have permissive signals for which he need not stop if they are red. The responsibility for avoiding a collision rests entirely with the hoghead of a following train when these kinds of block signals are in use, but he may not always have enough information to avoid an accident. The radio increases the information at his disposal to make judgments which could lead to a train wreck. However, silence on a railroad radio can foster misleading impressions of operating conditions.

Small portable radios are used by flagmen when they go out to flag approaching trains with their customary flagging equipment. These radios are also used at times by brakemen and switchmen when giving signals to the engineer while switching cars. Where three of these groundmen might formerly have been necessary to relay hand/lantern signals to an engineer around curves of industrial spurs or over great distances on straight track, now one man, with a radio, hanging on to the side of the lead car of a "shove" of a long cut of cars will ordinarily suffice.

The problem with the use of the radio to supplement hand/lantern signals in switching is that a man never knows when he has continuity of radio communication. A chance always exists that a few words will not be electronically transmitted to the person for whom they were intended. Furthermore, because rails rarely identify themselves in their radio messages during switching movements, a person could think "his man" is talking to him when in fact someone else's man is radioing "come ahead," "ten more car lengths to go," or "highball." Finally, a locomotive cab can be a very noisy place; a message properly sent by the correct man can be electronically received on the intended radio receiver but not properly understood or, at times, not even heard by the person for whom the message was transmitted.

The conductor and his rear man then chatted about another use of radio in railroading—radio control of *slave* diesel *units.* The parent O & W system and other carriers occasionally used a second set of "slave" diesel-electric units remotely located toward the middle or rear of a train. Traction motor power, dynamic braking, and air braking on the specially equipped slave units are controlled by the engineer via radio waves through supplementary controls in the specially equipped cab of his *master* diesel unit at the head of the train. As with any radio transmission, continuity of communication between the transmitter and the receiver cannot be insured. The two men recalled how one O & W engineer running a very long train with a set of master units and a remote set of slave units, had made an automatic brake application and shut off his throttle as he halted his train in order to comply with operating rules. Continuity of radio signal to his slave units had been lost and the fail-safe devices did not operate properly. His slave units attempted to master the train by pumping off the automatic air brakes and running with a wide open throttle setting. The unruly slaves derailed the rear of the train and caused great damage to the derailed cars.

HOTBOXES

Slim was working his five units at full throttle as the heavy UMX ground upgrade over Maxwell Mountain, known to the men as "the hill." He had a train order restricting him to 20 m.p.h. over the track a few miles up ahead.

Bob told him that a freight had "dropped a journal" there and caused some damage to the track which was not yet fully repaired by the gandies. The heavy UMX could not make more than 15 m.p.h. up the long grade anyway, so no speed reduction would be necessary.

As the UMX crawled along the damaged stretch of track, the student could see the chewed up ends of the wooden cross ties which had been cut by the flanges of the wheels on the derailed cars of the freight that had dropped its journal. He asked the head man about dropped journals. Bob explained in a loud voice above the tremendous roar of the diesels that all rolling stock moves on flanged steel wheels paired by heavy steel axles. The weight of the rolling stock is transferred to a wheel-axle assembly through bearings on the two ends of the axle. The bearing is called a journal. Almost all locomotives and passenger cars, and most newer freight cars, have roller bearings. Some locomotives and passenger cars, and many older freight cars, have solid brass journals housed in a lubricant-filled journal box in which the end of the axle rotates. At times, either roller or "solid" bearings fail mechanically and over-heat, causing a "hotbox." With solid bearings the hotbox usually causes a telltale odor and a column of dense smoke which comes from the burning lubricating oil of the hot journal box. Crews in cabs and in cabooses and em-ployees giving a train a roll by look for such telltale smoke. Roller bearings usually overheat less frequently, but give little visible warning of this condi-tion. Bob showed the student how to hold his hand over his nose in order to give the hand signal for a hotbox, which, if undetected, can lead to a derail-ment. Slim mentioned that Tom Potter had recently been running at 50 m.p.h. near Stone Creek and had suddenly derailed, scattering cars over the east- and westbound main line. It turned out that a roller bearing journal had failed on a car on his train.

Bob volunteered that he had had a hotbox in that same vicinity. As was customary, he was looking back out of the cab window inspecting the left-hand side of the train as they ran toward Dry River. He saw a column of dense smoke issuing from the third journal box of the eighth car behind the units. After the hoghead stopped the train, they put out the fire and began to move slowly to the nearest set-out track where they could leave the car off the main line, secured with its hand brake. The train moved only a short distance when the brass journal dropped out of its box. They almost had a derailment, but their vigilance and low speed kept them from derailing the car with its now frozen axle.

Bob continued his account by saying that after the flagman had been whistled out to protect the rear end of the train from any following trains, Bob radioed ahead to Dry River. The foreman of the car shop came to the site with a number of highway vehicles full of carmen and necessary equipment. They jacked up the "bad order" (defective) car with a heavy jack and removed the entire *truck* from the rear of the car. (A truck is the flexible, heavy steel frame bearing from one to four wheel-axle assemblies. Most rolling stock has two- or three-axle trucks. A truck is attached to and rotates beneath the un-derframe of a piece of rolling stock by means of a vertical center pin made of heavy steel.) The carmen rolled a new truck onto the rails, inserted a center pin, and jacked the car down onto the pin, which fits into an orifice in the underframe.

Bob finished by saying the foreman showed them that the car had a hotbox several times which each time had been allowed to cool. If the journal box had been inspected and rebuilt, they would not have experienced the close call. The car came from a northeastern carrier not noted for maintenance of its equipment. "That wooden axle outfit just loads their bad orders (defective cars) with freight and sends them west," Bob concluded.

After observing the next block signal, Slim remarked that on a recent trip a wayside hotbox-detecting device had alerted him with its flashing, white warning light. He stopped his train and read the instructions in the automatic hotbox detection device. Such detectors often sound false alarms because of hot brake shoes or other sources that originate false information. Was this a false alarm? Walking back along the train, the head brakeman found that a journal had dropped out of a hotbox just as the train had ground to a halt. "The hotbox detector paid for itself that time," said Slim. The student was told that like the radio, the detector was an aid to his work, but that he should not absolutely rely on the device.

"IT WAS ON THIS GRADE . . ."

As the UMX snaked through the curves of Apex station at the summit of Maxwell Mountain, Slim began to ease off on the throttle. He used the upgrade to brake his train, thus keeping his brake system fully charged for the downgrade ahead. "Bringing a train down this hill is an art," he said to Bob, who was still standing behind his seat after discussing the train orders with him. "When you make a heavy set, you don't dare release the brakes unless you've come to a stop." Such a release would most likely result in a runaway.

Bob thought of the lines of the song, "Old 97" (see Gamst 1975b:292):

> It was on this grade that he lost his average [air brake],
> You can see what a jump he made. . . .
> They found him in the wreck
> With his hand on the throttle, and a-scalded to death by the steam.

A runaway freight train is always a very real possibility on a mountain downgrade. (Runaway passenger trains on a downgrade have not occurred for a century or more in the United States, despite the popularity of this theme in folk songs such as "Old 97" and in Hollywood imagination.)

Using his locomotive brakes, Slim stopped the UMX at the east switch of Apex siding. The student lined the switch and motioned Slim ahead so that the UMX could run off the main line to allow No. 53 to pass them. "Look at the student's hand signal," he called down to Bob, who was now standing next to the student. "He is beginning to look like an old head after only a few student trips. In a few more weeks, he'll be telling me how to handle the train."

Freight eases down mountain grade on siding toward red signal as extra with produce for eastern markets labors upgrade on main line. It is late afternoon and white classification lights are easily seen.

Bob grinned up at the cab from his place on the ground. Standing next to the edge of the track, the head man and the student could smell all of the aromas of a hot day in a semi-arid setting. Foremost was the sharp, penetrating odor of the creosote oozing out of the sun-baked wooden ties. Fragrances of varying kinds emanated from the local plants; a sage-like bouquet was predominant. A dusty smell hung over the exceedingly dry soil along either side of the crushed rock ballast that held the cross ties to the ground. Intensifying all the olfactory stimuli was the intense dry heat which penetrated to the bones of anyone standing in it for long. The cab of the 2106 was not much cooler than along the track, but at least it afforded some shade. It would be better in the cab. Bob and the student swung up onto the front steps of the moving 2106 and entered the cab. "We'll follow the varnish (passenger train) down the hill to Piedmont," he remarked to the student, without telling him what "the varnish" meant.

The UMX would be limited by timetable rules to 15 m.p.h. during the initial part of the downgrade to Maxwell station, eight miles to the west, and then would be allowed to do 20 for the next 20 miles down to Piedmont. Lighter freight trains with fully operative dynamic, that is, electrical, brakes could begin the descent at 20 m.p.h. and then do as much as 35 down the last long leg of the grade, according to their tonnage. No. 53 would begin at 30, then do 40, and finally 50 m.p.h. down the steep grade. Passenger trains had superior air brake systems and, usually, a light enough tonnage that they could be controlled entirely with the dynamic braking system on the units.

The dynamic brake, it will be recalled, uses the energy of a moving train to rotate the locomotive wheels against the resistance of its axle-mounted traction motors. The engineer has temporarily converted the motors to electric generators by means of his controls. The train's motion or mechanical energy is transformed into electrical energy which is dissipated as heat through resistance grids mounted in a unit's roof.

While waiting for First 53 to pass, Bob and Slim conversed about a runaway freight train that had left the track on a curve on the Maxwell downgrade during World War II. "Those things don't happen *nowadays,* do they?" asked the student.

"Not as often as in those *olden* days," replied Bob, a bit malevolently.

The head man and the hoghead then "entertained" the student by discussing a recent runaway freight on Zenith Hill, which dominates the line from Jackson to Crofts. Pete Nash was hoghead on a heavy mineral train of 8600 tons, the GBX—the Gypsum Board. Unknown to him, five of his cars had inoperative brakes that had been cut out by carmen during mechanical repairs, and twenty-six cars had defective brakes. The piston travel of the brake cylinder under each of the twenty-six cars was too great, thus causing poor braking.

Cresting the summit of the hill at Zenith station, Nash found he could not control his train with the usual combination of dynamic and automatic air brake systems. (Only two units out of his "mix-match" of six had effective dynamic brakes.) As the speedometer needle crept up near the point of runaway (beyond which no braking system would retard them as they accelerated downgrade), he became concerned. Pete could not afford the time to study his situation. He decided to "plug it" (put train into emergency). Otherwise he and his crew members would have to "join the birds" (jump off the moving train).

Nash pulled his automatic brake valve lever as far as it would go in a counterclockwise direction, into the emergency notch (position) on the quadrant of his 5-position brake valve. He had "wiped the clock." The sound of compressed air exploded into the cab as he set off the braking impulse that in rapid succession moved the brake control valve beneath each unit and car into its emergency position. Under each car, the control valve diverts compressed air from the emergency section of a two-part reservoir to the brake cylinder, the piston of which is forced out under great pressure. This pressure is exerted through steel brake levers and rods to iron brake shoes forced against each wheel. Control valve, air reservoir, brake cylinder, and brake rigging are usually suspended from beneath a car's underframe. The brake pipe pressure would now continue to vent to the atmosphere until the normal pressure of 90 p.s.i. in the automatic brake system would reach 0. By this time, each car brake cylinder would have its full emergency pressure of 77 p.s.i. multiplied through the brake levers and then exerted upon the steel brake beams mounted at right angles to the wheels and holding the brake shoes. Seldom in his long career had Pete Nash had to release such high braking forces on a moving train. (A hoghead might plug a stopped train before switching nearby in order to keep it from rolling away.)

The GBX continued to plunge down the mountain grade of over 2 percent. Its speedometer needle crept upward rapidly—well above authorized speed—30, 35, 40, 45, and then 50 m.p.h. Eventually, the speed reached 60 m.p.h. and held for two miles. At last, Nash slowed and finally stopped the GBX on the steep grade, after running almost out of control for seven miles. When Pete had his brake system recharged, he "doubled down the hill," taking one-half of his train down at a time. Taking the rear half of the train down on the second trip, he made a service reduction of his brake pipe of 10 p.s.i. and then he made the full service reduction of 26 p.s.i., the greatest he could make before having to go into emergency again. The speed once more had begun to creep up rapidly. With a full service reduction, he had 64 p.s.i. in his car brake cylinders. However, as he watched the speedometer needle creep alarmingly up the dial, he realized he would have to plug it again in order to stop to let No. 53 pass him. Later on, going down to join the front half of his train, he had to go into emergency a third time.

Nash left 18 cars of crushed rock at Orwell, at the base of Zenith Hill, and held the GBX down to 15–20 m.p.h. on the remainder of the run to Crofts. The GBX was left at Crofts for about a week and only a few of its loads at a time were sent on to Urbana in various trains. Many of the cars needed new iron brake shoes at Crofts because they had been burned down through three inches of thickness to the shoe holders on the brake beams.

"Zenith Hill is not quite as steep as Maxwell Mountain, but it can be deceptive," said Bob. He recalled to the others the time that a Granger Railroad baggage car in No. 17, the *Fast Mail,* had a hotbox on Zenith Hill. The mail train was stopped, the hotbox fire extinguished, and then the car (containing express packages, storage mail, and a corpse in a coffin) was switched onto a set-out track by the passenger locomotive of No. 17. While the passenger units were coupling back on to the train and the air brake, air signal, and steam heating lines were being recoupled, the baggage car rolled from the set-out track and took off down Zenith Hill. The heat of the fire had damaged an air pressure gauge inside the car and the air in the brake cylinder had leaked from the gauge until the car brakes released. Accelerating downgrade created a draft on the rekindled fire in the 60-foot, 60-ton baggage car, which was burned down to its heavy steel underframe and trucks by the time it reached the bottom of the hill. "The company not only transports corpses, it also cremates them enroute as part of its service," cracked Bob to the student.

DOWN THE HILL

After the passage of First 53, which carried green signals for a second section running—as directed through train orders by the dispatcher—two hours behind schedule, the UMX crawled out of the passing track onto the main line. It then crested the grade and began the descent of one of the most difficult stretches of main line in North America. Slim began to bunch the mineral train with his dynamic brake. The amperage indicating meter did not climb steadily, as expected, when he increased the braking force by pulling back on the lever. The indicator fluctuated a bit and he felt the dynamic braking force fade. His units continued to whine loudly and the diesel engines chanted a modest amount. Both sounds were normal.

As usual, Slim would have to make a judgment on the amount of automatic air brake reduction he required in conjunction with the dynamic. Part of the judgment concerned the kinds of cars and the tonnage behind his units, as well as the condition of the dynamic. Slim thought about both. The dynamic was not very good at the moment, but was not too abnormal considering the mix-match of five different units that he had. As for the cars, auto-carrying cars and trailer-carrying flat cars—both kinds are 85 feet long—did not brake well. And, on a downgrade like this, tank cars sloshed their liquid cargo, and heavily laden mineral cars often had the characteristics of rolling boulders. Normally doing 10 to 12 m.p.h. down out of Apex, the hoghead would make a reduction of 8 to 10 p.s.i. with his automatic brake valve. He would then lessen or increase the force of the dynamic, by reading his amperage meter, in order to keep his speed constant with his reduction of air. At times, he would have to make a further reduction of "several more pounds" so that he could easily control the heavy train with a dynamic.

After a "twelve pound reduction," in two phases 20 seconds apart, Slim's speed was creeping up over the required 15 m.p.h. that he was trying to maintain with his units whining loudly in dynamic operation; they were braking even more poorly than he had first thought. A further reduction in his brake pipe was necessary. Compressed air roared into the cab, as he moved his automatic brake valve lever further along the self-lapping service part of its quadrant. His air gauges showed 74 p.s.i., or a "sixteen pound reduction" for the brake pipe. Velocity continued to increase on their descent. Next he added to the total braking force by using the third of his four braking systems, the locomotive's independent air brakes. These were not supposed to be used in conjunction with the dynamic brakes except when coming to a stop, but they were needed now to regulate the downgrade speed around his "heavy set" of automatic air brakes on the train. Speed was still creeping up. Slim gently pulled his locomotive air brake lever counterclockwise on its quadrant and allowed his locomotive brake cylinder pressure to build up very gradually. He finally got things under control and in equilibrium between 14 and 16 m.p.h. It was a difficult and heavy train.

"Well, I guess I don't have to pull the air on you, *this time,*" Bob joked, as he playfully fingered the handle of the emergency brake valve in front of him on the left-hand side of the cab. "I thought I was going to have to take appropriate action to see that you complied with the rules."

"I was about to whistle out a 'call for hand brakes.' Then you and Teddy and Eddie could 'decorate,' (climb out on the tops of the cars) and tie down hand brakes to help me hold back this train," replied Slim, a bit irritated and only half joking. He was referring to the fourth braking system—the mechanical hand brake found on each piece of rolling stock—sometimes used when all else fails. Until the advent of air brake systems in the late nineteenth century, brakemen slowed and stopped trains by hand braking the cars of a train. Since the 1960s, crew members no longer walk the top of a train.

If the train did not handle properly, Slim said he would indeed stop at Maxwell and have the trainmen set by hand the *retainers* on each car. A retainer is a small lever-operated valve mounted near the hand brake wheel on every car. When it is set, the retainer controls the rate of exhaust of a car's brake cylinder air. Bob explained to the student that it was a lot of work to climb on the cars to set retainers for descending a grade and then release them afterward at the base of the grade. However, he allowed that they were necessary when the engineer had difficulty controlling a heavy train. By holding a preset amount of brake cylinder pressure, even when the brakes are released by the engineer, the retainers prevent speed from increasing too rapidly while the engineer recharges his air brake system during a downgrade run. Use of retainers is mandatory on trains with particularly heavy tonnages, inoperative or poor dynamic brakes, or when an 18 p.s.i. reduction in the brake pipe is necessary to control a train's descent. If retainers are used all the way out of Apex, the steel wheels of the cars can overheat from the constant braking, and wheel fractures can occur. To prevent this dangerous possibility, a ten-minute cooling stop must be made two-thirds of the way down the grade. For the same reasons similar cooling stops must be made on Zenith Hill.

If Slim had any further problems, he would have to halt his train; he did not dare release his train brakes and attempt to recharge his train line while moving downgrade. He would not use more than 18 p.s.i. of reduction to balance the speed of his train because he needed the remaining 8 p.s.i. to stop the train if necessary. (Below 26 p.s.i. with a 90 p.s.i. train line [brake pipe], no additional reduction of air pressure will result in further buildup of brake cylinder pressure in a trailing car. Such a car now has equalized pressures between its air reservoir and its brake cylinder.) If he did stop to recharge, Slim would need hand brakes set on the train to hold it before he moved his automatic brake valve into release position. By doing so the train line could be recharged to 90 p.s.i. from his main air reservoirs on each unit. Increasing brake pipe pressure actuates a car's control valve to cause the car brake cylinder to exhaust its air and release its pressure on the brake shoes. It could take quite a few minutes to recharge a train line, especially if a full 26 p.s.i. reduction had been made to stop the train, and if the train line had excessive leakage, as it sometimes did.

At Maxwell, the grade temporarily tapers off before plunging again toward Piedmont. Lighter trains sometimes stall here on their automatic brake application. Care must be exercised in preventing a train from stalling. If the forward end of a train is allowed to run too fast in relation to the rear end, the flexible steel knuckle or the steel shank (drawbar) of a coupler of one of the cars will break because of the severe strain upon it of pull from the front and retardation from the rear. An area near Maxwell is called "drawbar flats" because this level area in the grade has caused many drawbars to pull out, often because the train has not been properly handled. But Slim had so much tonnage that he was able to ease off slowly on his locomotive brakes and use the weak dynamic to keep his speed at about 15 m.p.h. through Maxwell and its flats.

The hoghead had to be aware of many factors at once: his timetable and train order restrictions on his right to occupy the main line, the block signals and other wayside signals, men along the track, and his running dynamics, or mechanical forces of motion. These dynamics included his speed and the variation of the binding of curves and steepness of grade. He had to keep an eye on the strength of his electrical (dynamic) brakes, and he had to remember that if he used his locomotive air brakes very much he would overheat the locomotive wheels. The amount of brake pipe reduction in relation to the total permissible and possible service reductions of the automatic air brakes had to be constantly kept in mind. Moreover, he could not apply a braking system or power from the throttle without thinking of how it would affect the trailing cars, their cargoes, and the crew members in the caboose who are sometimes joined by company officers or other employees traveling on company business. If he used the dynamic or independent locomotive brakes too abruptly, he would cause a strong run-in of the slack, or play, in the train and thus damage cargo and possibly injure the men on the caboose. Should he release either of these two brakes suddenly, he would allow the slack to run out too quickly, with the same results, and possibly "get a knuckle or a drawbar." Ahead, the downgrade continued for many miles.

Slim uses a split initial reduction in the automatic brake system when slowing a train, with a twenty-second interval between the two phases. This practice allows the brake shoes to begin to retard slightly the forward motion of the wheels. The second phase of the braking effort is thus not effective until slack has had a chance to be controlled in the train by gently running it in against the locomotive. Besides reading his air brake gauges, conditions of various systems of his units must be monitored by means of gauges and color-coded lights. For example, certain electrical problems cause a purple or a white light to be illuminated, accompanied by a jangling alarm bell. The hoghead's mind must always be ahead several blocks on the track and back along his train. Questions like, What situation am I approaching? and Is my train bunched or stretched? must be on his mind at all times. He must know the minor fluctuations in gradient and changes in alignment of the roadbed so that he can handle the train properly rather than having the train handle him.

Slim had his mind on two lesser stretches of drawbar flats on the line below Maxwell, when, unexpectedly, the white wheel-slip light flashed on and the dynamic brake surged down to a lower amperage. The wheels of his units had slipped in some oily deposit from track-mounted oilers for train wheel flanges. These are at various locations and are used to reduce wear on curved rail caused by the wheel flanges of cars as they scream in the tight bond of a curve. When the wheels slip, the dynamic brake loses some of its power and the train speed increases. If further automatic air brake reduction is made to hold speed constant, the train will begin to slow and stall when the dynamic regains its strength. Coming out of a curve, Slim used heavier dynamic and locomotive air brakes to eat away gradually at his now excessive speed of 20

Engineer snags train orders. Lower set of orders is for caboose.

m.p.h. The UMX plunged across a bridge spanning a dry wash and entered a cut along a hillside. All along the side of the train a moderate haze of grayish white smoke issued from the hot wheels of the cars. Anyone standing beside the track would be able to detect the stench of hot steel. From a greater distance, the train would appear as a long snake with smoking flanks, sparks flying from its nostrils (the diesel exhaust stacks), and a bright single eye (the headlight).

At last they were approaching Piedmont and the tower at the west end of Piedmont yard gave them a succession of restrictive block signals. Slim kept the UMX tightly bunched as his units rolled through the busy yard with most of his train still on the mountain grade behind him. Running by the Piedmont depot at the required 10 m.p.h., the UMX approached the train order mast to the left of the track. Bob snagged their train orders from the forked arm that held a wide loop of heavy white cord, with the clearance and orders tied in a tight knot of the cord. Bob's arm had speared through the open loop which easily left the forked arm attached to the train order mast. As Slim rolled the UMX toward the highway overpass beyond the train order mast, he finished easing off on the dynamic brake and made the changes on his levers for powering his traction motors, which had been used as braking generators all the way down the Maxwell grade. He waited 10 seconds and then slowly opened the throttle one notch every 3 or 4 seconds. The UMX began to stretch out as the diesel engines chanted louder. With each notch of the throttle, they delivered more horsepower to spin the main generators which powered the traction motors turning the locomotive's wheels. Slim's attention was again all along his accelerating train and ahead toward conditions on the right of way which were yet to be encountered.

SETTING OUT

The UMX headed for Groveton Tower. The crew had a number of cars to set out at Groveton, where they would be forwarded to distant terminals by another carrier. Groveton is a car interchange point (just as Piedmont is) between the CC & U and another railroad. Single cars, large cuts of cars, or even entire trains are handed over from one carrier to another at innumerable interchange tracks throughout the country. A car loaded on one railroad might run across several more before being spotted at the site of its consignee. Cars of United States, Canadian, and Mexican railroads are, in a word, interchangeable.

After going by a double yellow at Groveton Tower, which controlled the crossing with the other carrier, the UMX ran parallel to its set-out track. Slim was stopping the train stretched under power. After making his automatic reduction, he kept the handle depressed on his independent brake valve, thus keeping locomotive brakes released while train brakes were applying. Gradually, he eased off on the throttle to prevent excessive amperage, and hence tractive effort, from building up as the train speed decreased. Too much tractive effort could strain and then part his long, heavy train by pulling out a drawbar.

After making a second reduction on his automatic train brakes and coming to a stop at Groveton, a total 20 p.s.i. reduction was made to hold the UMX on the main line. Then with the units he "doubled over" the lead cars of the train to other cars already on the set-out track. The brakemen guided the units back to the train waiting on the main line, with only the first six cars still next to the rear unit. These were the loads of cement picked up at Cementon and destined for the metropolitan Urbana area, where the cargo would go into all manner of construction.

After the brakemen had put the UMX back together again, and the proper air brake test was made, the hoghead began accelerating toward Union Tower, some six miles away from Groveton Tower. Yard locomotives were bustling about Groveton Yard. They would soon distribute the cars set out by the UMX to a number of trains going to different terminals on that foreign carrier. Busy yardmasters were filling out trains within tonnage limits; they had their own mountains to contend with. Roundhouse foremen were readying units, crew dispatchers were calling crews, and the chief train dispatcher of the foreign carrier was lining up train movements for the next eight hours. How light, and thus how fast, should he make the time freights and how heavy should he make the slower trains which would do "the chores" along the line of setting out and picking up cars. Far to the west in Urbana Yard, a CC & U roundhouse foreman desperately wanted Slim's units. Urbana yardmasters were anticipating the arrival of his heavy carloads of minerals.

Sitting on a pick-up track at Groveton was a long cut of new, bright orange, mechanical "reefers" (refrigerator cars) loaded with fresh produce destined for eastern markets. Their diesel-generator cooling units hummed in the sunlit quiet of the day. The eastbound Advanced Eastern Exchange (AEX) would pick them up in an hour or so. Since September 1973, the railroads no longer provide block-ice service for the older kind of reefers, which were actually iceboxes on wheels. About a century ago these older refrigerator cars revolutionized agricultural distribution and hence all of American agriculture. In the dripping, wooden, iced cars fresh fruits and vegetables (and later dressed meat) could be shipped from western and southern farms to distant, populous metropolitan centers. American railroads and agriculture were off to a profitable partnership and American urban households changed from a diet of dry staples to one of nutritious, fresh, in-season produce. The traditional orange in a child's Christmas stocking is a survival from the pre-reefer-era in railroading—a time when oranges were a relatively uncommon and expensive luxury good. Declining produce traffic on railroads could be entirely lost to trucks by the end of the 1980s.

Rolling down the main line, Slim received a red over green signal at Union Tower. He was cleared through a diverging route to Union City on the way to Urbana. Allowable speed was 30 m.p.h. through the interlocking plant and then 20 m.p.h. past Union City depot, a large, ornate building. Already his speed was down for the restricted stretches of track. The hoghead could have made a very light brake pipe reduction of about 6 p.s.i. much earlier to reduce his speed. However, such a light reduction would allow some brake control valves under some cars to "kick off" their brakes. Further, when he went to release the light brake application, many of the car brakes would remain stuck and would not be able to release. Consequently, the hoghead had used a 9 p.s.i. reduction in order to obviate any problems with his automatic brake system. However, he had to release the brakes before his speed dropped too low and the UMX began to stall. Pulling against a very slowly moving train with brakes still releasing would cause his powerful units to pull out a drawbar somewhere back along the cars.

The operator-agent at Union City depot rolled them by as Slim munched on the sandwich he had purchased at the Crofts beanery ages ago. He should have purchased two, or even four, he thought, now that he was good and hungry. Bob gave him an apple. And they all enjoyed the student's coffee as they wound slowly through Union City on to the single track main line to Urbana Yard. The centralized traffic control dispatcher was himself sipping his coffee as he monitored on his CTC console their entrance into his territory. He lined them up with clear block signals along the single track for a number of miles.

The crew of the UMX had now been on duty for eight hours. Rule 88 of the engineer's labor contract between the Brotherhood of Locomotive Engineers (BLE) and the CC & U reads: "Engineers in through freight will be allowed time for a meal when they have been on duty five hours and it is apparent the trip cannot be completed within eight hours . . ." The brakemen and conductors (and remaining firemen) have a similar rule in their respective contracts, held by the United Transportation Union (UTU). In 1969, a unification of the former Order of Railway Conductors and Brakemen, Brotherhood of Locomotive Firemen and Enginemen, Brotherhood of Railroad Trainmen, and the Switchmen's Union of North America resulted in the UTU, an AFL-CIO affiliate. The BLE and UTU are the only two trade unions extant for on-train operating employees. Given the wording of their labor agreements, the crew members of the UMX could have "gone to beans" at

Piedmont or Groveton, but chose, instead, to "run their beans" and get home.

Had the dispatcher controlling the Maxwell Mountain line delayed them very much, or had their new dispatcher arranged an unanticipated chore for them enroute to Urbana, the crew would react and tell the dispatcher, "We're going to beans! Have the yardmaster at Piedmont clear a track to hold us!"

7/The home terminal

In this chapter we complete the run presented in the previous two chapters and turn to other aspects of a rail's life. These aspects include important parts of the value system of a railroader. Values are beliefs concerning what is appropriate and inappropriate behavior in a particular situation. Ethnological study invariably focuses upon values even if the beliefs are not specifically labeled as such by the researcher. We learn of a rail's reaction to people seen along the right of way and also to a dangerous tank truck on a grade crossing. Railroaders very much value family life, perhaps all the more because many of its psychic satisfactions are denied to them due to the restraints of the job. In some ways, the brothers of the various operating crafts form a very large surrogate family whose members are present for as many as five decades. These "family" members are disciplined by the group when they misbehave and are mourned when they die or are killed, all in accordance with the railroaders' values.

HEADING HOME

On a succession of green eyes, the UMX moved through the suburban landscape west of Union City. The next two siding-stations, Weyburn and Applegate, were less than one mile apart. Some of the sidings out in the wilderness east of Jackson were ten or more miles apart. Rail traffic was denser in the heavily populated megalopolis sprawling from Piedmont to beyond Urbana. A local freight was "in the hole" for them at Weyburn siding. Apparently, the "delayer" did not want the UMX to "go in the hole for beans" somewhere east of Urbana Yard. The local had been diverted into the siding sufficiently in advance so that the UMX did not get even one restrictive block signal.

Having passed the last color-light block signal with its green indication, Slim found it was still imprinted in the retina of his eye. The wayside telegraph poles of the company marched in endless procession to the horizon. The further the UMX went, the more wooden soldiers that appeared to join the endless ranks of poles. Outside of the railroad property, just beyond the telegraph poles, were the backyards of America. Trackside vistas are not of the fronts of houses, prepared for public viewing, but of the normally hidden and private backs of houses. The curtains usually are not drawn across the windows, and housewives can be seen through rear kitchen windows preparing a meal, sometimes gazing vacantly at the rolling freights. Their children often wave as they halt their play to give a train an unwitting roll by. Crew members wave back at them. It used to be a friendly return gesture, but now it is often "so the little bastards don't throw any rocks through our windows," as Bob had once remarked. The bric-a-brac of industrial civilization is strewn across patios and backyards: an old junk auto which will never be repaired, a wooden planked boat needing paint and caulking, scrap boards under an open shed, and a children's swing set on its rusting A-frame.

Dogs also note the passing trains and bark at the movement that rumbles past and trembles the ground. Sometimes they run excitedly in circles in their fenced yard as a train roars by. At dusk the glow of television tubes emanates from the darkened but unshaded rear rooms of houses. Poorer families have the bluish white glow of black and white television; those better off bask in the brighter, golden glow of their color sets. Summer is always "prime viewing time" for the passing train crews. That's when they get to see women sunbathing or at the side of backyard swimming pools. "Jimmy, will you look at that gal! When old Butler comes by in the caboose, he'll fall out of the cupola from staring so hard. Of course, that's all he's good for. Wow! Look at the legs on that one!"

The usually screened back lots of American industry are also viewable from trains. A factory or warehouse often has an impressive façade facing the public on its street frontage. But behind the building are open-sided structures and piles of materials. The unimpressive inventory of American industry is inadvertently displayed for the eyes of train crews—stacks of lumber, coils of sheet steel, piles of bricks, heaps of sand, rolls of cable, braced tiers of pipe, and disarrays of odds and ends too valuable to discard immediately.

Industry and commerce necessarily have their unmasked back open to the rail lines and their probing spurs: steel mills, coal mines, lumber yards, automobile assembly plants, sand and gravel pits, textile mills, department store and supermarket warehouses, canneries, and produce packing houses— all have their well-being intertwined with that of the railroad. Freight trains are an extension of the assembly line and of storage inventory of a business firm. Delays or stoppages of rail freight service mean corresponding delays and stoppages soon will follow for line-side firms.

Just past Applegate, the units of the UMX suddenly lurched and power dropped as the driving wheels slipped on the rails of a rough spot on the track, which had become rougher with a recent heavy rain. The heart of each of the crew members in the cab of the 2106 pounded very rapidly. A locomotive engineer trainee had recently hit such a rough spot running at 12 m.p.h. between Cementon and Apex with another UMX, and the sudden surge of the train had broken both coupler knuckles between the second and third cars behind the units. One of the knuckles showed about 50 percent old fracture along its broken edge. Luckily, Slim's UMX remained in one piece. Slim

With two units disabled and alarm bells ringing, an extra crawls into siding after delaying first section of second class freight, whose head man stands next to dispatcher's phone booth. View is from cab of delayed train, holding the main line.

reflexively made an automatic brake reduction to save the rear-end crew from being flung around in the cupola by the sag in the track.

An alarm bell started ringing in the cab of the 2106. Slim turned his head and torso around 180° from his line of sight out the front cab window in order to view the rear wall of his cab. On the rear wall is the diesel engine control panel with its emergency stop button, various operating controls, and a number of color-coded warning lights which monitor conditions of the diesel and of the locomotive unit proper. He scanned the lights. None were illuminated. The problem was not on the 2106 then, but on one or more of the trailing units. The alarm lights and indicating gauges of trailing units are not repeated on the lead/control unit; only the alarm bell is relayed into the lead cab. Slim had ample power with his remaining units for the rolling hills before him. He would let the alarm bell ring for a while.

In the days when he had a fireman-helper to assist him he would have sent the fireman back to trouble-shoot the problem. (Brakemen are not trained to trouble-shoot diesel-electrics.) If the power reduction were severe enough, Slim would have stopped the train and gone back to correct the problem himself. Slim could recall times grinding upgrade from Piedmont to Apex at 4 m.p.h. with two of four units malfunctioning. Both he and his fireboy were back on the running boards of the disabled units trouble-shooting and trying to get them both back "on the line." Up in the cab, the head man sat in the hoghead's seat so that he could depress the *deadman* foot pedal. If the pedal is allowed to spring upward, a penalty brake application takes place and all power is cut off to the traction motors. At 4 m.p.h., the head man had ample time to recall the hoghead by whistle before any change in throttle setting was necessary. Of course, it had been a violation of the operating rules for either, let alone *both*, enginemen to be on the running board of units in motion. Realistically, if the train were to stall on the steep grade, they might never start it again with only two operable units.

After traversing most of the seven miles to Oxford siding, Slim received ever more restrictive block signals from the centralized traffic control (CTC) dispatcher. The double signal governing the track switch at the east end of Oxford siding and the main line was red over lunar and the dispatcher had lined the motorized track switch for the siding. "Heading in," Bob called the signal as soon as he saw it about a mile ahead.

"Lunar—heading in," Slim responded.

The student stirred somewhat in the former "fireman's seat." Bob told him to relax. The dispatcher had lined the track switch into the siding and would line them out on the west end, 6000 feet ahead, when he would give them a green dwarf signal to leave the siding and enter the single track main line, remote controlled by CTC. The electronic wonder of CTC increases the capacity of any line and allows faster schedules because meets and passes between trains are often running ones. Seldom is a train stopped for long. CTC on a single track line gives it about 75 percent of the capacity of *double track* (two assigned directions of traffic with automatic block signals, ABS. On *two main tracks* (no assigned direction of traffic), CTC has about the capacity of triple track controlled by ABS.

When Slim had the UMX stopped several car lengths short of the absolute red dwarf signal, he applied fully his locomotive brakes and released and began recharging his train brakes. Now with the train stopped, and the locomotive brakes applied he could remove his foot from the deadman pedal without causing a penalty brake application and the white pneumatic control warning light to burn. Slim walked back along his units to find the cause of the alarm bell. The second unit from the rear was the culprit. Its diesel engine was dead and it was deathly quiet, except for the alarm bell.

The purple "no power" and the yellow "engine governor shut down" lights were illuminated. Opening the high voltage cabinet doors on the rear cab wall of the unit, which were marked "DANGER 600 VOLTS," Slim turned the oval doorknob-like isolation switch from RUN to ISOLATE. The inter-unit alarm bell ceased its din. The quiet felt good to his ears. If the red "hot engine" light had been illuminated, the bell would not have been quieted. He checked the white "ground relay" light. It was not illuminated.

Next, Slim went out of the cab through its rear door behind the vacant engineer's workplace and stepped down onto the running board extending the length of the long engine room hood. He unlatched and opened a middle door and located the governor on the huge diesel engine and pressed the engine governor button back into its operating position. The engine's overspeed trip needed resetting and he pulled it toward him, latching it into operating position. No more than the usual leakage of crankcase oil was visible on the engine room floor. He then put the engine start switch in the engine room in PRIME position and waited until he saw fuel oil flowing through a sight glass mounted on the diesel. The hoghead pulled about one-third of the way on the long manual control lever of the diesel's fuel injectors and turned and held the start switch in START position. The diesel rumbled and sputtered and then coughed as the heavy unit trembled while its ten-ton main generator powered by storage batteries housed under the cab was used as a starting motor. As the generator continued to crank, the diesel surged into a dull roar and dense smoke belched out of the exhaust stacks penetrating the roof. Slim released the start switch and gradually released the injector control lever as the diesel began to run at idle speed.

Returning to the cab of the now murmuring unit, Slim placed the isolation switch in RUN. Now the unit was back "on the line" and would respond to calls for tractive power and dynamic braking from the controls on the 2106. The wheel slippage on the rough track had killed the diesel on the trailing unit. It should now stay on the line. Sometimes the trouble-shooting was more complex and a cantankerous unit would not restart, or stay started, or stay on the line when power was demanded of it.

An eastbound time freight had roared and rumbled by while Slim was trouble-shooting on the disabled unit. By the time he had returned to the cab of the 2106 the dwarf signal was green. He whistled two longs (release brakes; proceed) and prepared to resume the run home. Now he was really getting hungry.

Rounding a high-speed curve at 50 m.p.h., Slim and Bob both picked up immediately an object on the tracks about a mile ahead on a highway grade crossing. The student, although vigilant and observing the track ahead as he was supposed to do, did not detect the lethal silhouette with his all-seeing eyes. The object was the grayish-silver, semicylindrical form of a tank truck, many of which transport gasoline or other dangerous liquids. Already the UMX had covered one-fifth of the distance to the crossing along the slight downgrade of the railroad line. Automatic air sounded loudly in the cab and Slim also began to reduce his throttle to idle. Bob was radioing the crew in the caboose to "hold on"; the slack in the train was about to run in somewhat abruptly. The tank truck still seemed welded to the highway crossing. Why didn't it move? What was the driver doing? If the UMX hit a gasoline truck at any moderate or high speed, the vehicle would explode into a massive fireball and, at the very least, burning gasoline would penetrate every crevice of the cab.

With only a quarter of a mile to go and the train speed down to 35 m.p.h., the truck at last lurched off the crossing and down the other side of the embankment of the crossing. The driver, as is often the case, had trouble shifting gears after coming to a complete stop while attempting to cross railroad tracks located on an embankment several feet higher than the level of the highway crossing it. The head end crew relaxed their knotted stomach muscles, and Slim released his white bloodless fingers from the right-hand armrest of his seat. As is customary, the two veteran railroaders did not verbalize their own momentary fears.

Grade crossing impacts with gasoline or chemical trucks are among the worst nightmares of railroaders and are a topic of frequent discussion. The National Transportation Safety Board (NTSB) recognizes the severity of the problem and is working on solutions. One of the Railroad Accident Reports of the NTSB poignantly reports on the impact of a gasoline truck and a passenger train (NTSB 1971a:18):

The cause of fatalities to engine crewmembers and the official was the entrance of burning gasoline into the [cab] and engine [room] compartments which burned the occupants of the [cab], made escape into the engine compartment useless, and forced the occupants to jump from the [cab] while the train was still moving at a speed too high to insure survival.

In still another such accident the NTSB explains (NTSB1977b:11):

Both occupants of the locomotive cab were killed instantly. With visibility [in fog on a 90 m.p.h. train] estimated at less than 700 feet, the enginemen [engineer and fireman] were probably unaware of the impending collision [with an oil truck] until about 5 seconds before it occurred. As there was no derailment and the collision impact did not greatly reduce the speed of the train, the enginemen probably were killed by the flaming oil which entered the cab. Both the outer and inner nose compartment doors were insufficiently secured to resist the impact and explosive ignition of the oil. Both were blown inward off their hinges and with the broken cab windows permitted immediate and massive entry of flaming oil into the cab.

ARRIVAL AT URBANA TERMINAL

About a mile east of Urbana Yard, Slim began to bunch his decelerated train with the dynamic brake. The alarm bell was ringing again for a trailing unit. Well in advance, the dispatcher had lined the switches and block signals for one of the long receiving tracks for inbound, through-freight trains. The yardmaster and the roundhouse foreman, who by now had only two units at his disposal, were waiting for the UMX. An outbound freight, the *Advance Eastern Exchange,* eased past the UMX at 5 m.p.h., on a second main line. When the caboose of the UMX cleared a block signal bridge to the rear, the dispatcher would be able to line up a route onto the single track for the eastbound AEX. It would run to Groveton to pick up the waiting refrigerator cars. Then the AEX would go on to Piedmont, over Maxwell Mountain, down to Dry River, and through the junction to Crofts at JN Tower. Six hours from now a crew laying over at Crofts would be in the company beanery awaiting the arrival of the eastbound train to take to their home terminal at Jackson.

After running his units to the roundhouse, Slim walked over to the long, low, barracks-like building housing the enginemen's register room, locker room, and shower-wash-toilet area. Slim sat on one of the benches on either side of the long table in the register room, and registered in. TRAIN "UMX;" ENGINE UNITS "2106;" ENGINEER "ROGERS;" FIREMAN "————;" TIME OF ARRIVAL—AT DESIGNATED MAIN TRACK SWITCH "8:05P," AT DESIGNATED RELIEVING TRACK "8:20P;" REST HAD PREVIOUS TO LAST RUN"————;" LENGTH OF TIME ON LAST RUN "9:30."

Across from Slim sat Timmy "Gorilla" Gardner who had just registered out for the *Eastern Exchange* (EX). Slim related some of the highlights of his run to his powerfully built friend of almost thirty years. The conversation turned to Maxwell Hill. Timmy said that some "crazy fool" had shot a rifle at his train between Apex and Maxwell on his last trip. "It was bad enough with them Goddamn kids throwing rocks at us. Now we're being shot at," he stormed. Several train crew members had been hit in recent years by stones thrown by children. "Rocking" of trains was becoming more common and dangerous all the time, and cab windows could not withstand the impact of large, heavy rocks dropped or thrown in the path of a train from an overpass. At any time the series of injuries from rocking could be lethally punctuated with the death of any one of them.

Slim changed to a more pleasant topic of conversation, while Timmy waited for his units, three of which would be from those just brought in on the UMX. Slim noted that, "almost every trip a train of the J S & Z [railroad which shares some trackage with the CC & U] bogs down on the hill and ties things up. Seems like their power is falling apart. And they have had several units run out of fuel lately. Apparently they don't have much supervision, either." He concluded with a comparison of the management of the two neighboring carriers. This had been his first trip in several without being stuck behind a J S & Z freight that had ground to a halt on the grade. Timmy said that he had similar experiences with the J S & Z.

Gardner asked his friend if he had heard about the runaway car of the previous day on Maxwell Hill. Slim replied that he had not. Timmy said in a very even tone that it was "a bad one." A flat car with an old style staff hand brake, which is difficult to operate and requires a brake club (a wooden staff) for its proper operation, "got away" at Westerly about ten miles downgrade to the east of Apex. The conductor and a brakeman from the J S & Z train that was switching the flat car, loaded with about 50 tons of lumber, seized the grab irons on the sides of the car and swung up onto it so that they could stop it with the hand brake.

The two groundmen could not even slow the flat of lumber with the staff brake, Timmy related. The engineer on the J S & Z locomotive chased the load and attempted to couple into the accelerating car at 40 m.p.h., but the knuckles on the automatic couplers of the locomotive and those of the car would not couple. After realigning the couplers, a second attempt was made to capture the runaway, which was still accelerating on the downgrade. When the engineer hit the flat car, he was going 60 m.p.h. and, at that point, the load of lumber shifted on the level deck of the car, throwing both men from their precarious perches onto the ground. Both lost their lives trying to prevent a possible disaster further down the line toward Cementon.

A short time prior to this incident, brakeman Norm Holland did not lose his life, but lost a leg: When hanging from the side of a car being shoved over a grade crossing near Kingston, he was hit by a truck.

"On this job you never know from one day to the next," Slim said, in the customary fatalistic manner.

Switchman applies staff brake, by hand, on a flat car. (Hand) grab iron and (foot) U-shaped stirrup is at forward side of car.

MILEAGE, OTHER GOOD, AND PROTECTION OF GOOD

The term "good," in this section, is used in the sense employed by George M. Foster and other ethnologists, to mean the desired things in life. Good includes wealth, status, power, influence, security, safety, manliness, honor, respect, friendship, and, for rails, seniority and mileage to be earned. Briefly stated, this term connotes that which promotes success, welfare, or happiness and which leads to the advancement of self- or group-interest.

Slim recorded the miles he had made on his trip to and from Crofts on the proper form provided by the Brotherhood of Locomotive Engineers (BLE). The forms were located on a special desk near the register table. The local division of his union, representing CC & U engineers from Urbana to Crofts, regulates the number of miles earned per month by the men and prevents any individual from taking more than his allocated share. Some men dream of earning more miles, and a few, known as "sharpshooters" (basically, rails who take good not rightfully their own at the expense of others in their occupational group) scheme to earn more by various stratagems and misrepresentations of fact. Those known as being "mile hungry" merely covet and unduly preoccupy themselves with matters of mileage, but are not outright breakers of the rails' code of social etiquette of work.

Sharpshooters and those hungry for miles are countered and checked in various ways in order to protect the two central goods of operating railroaders. These two goods are an allocation of mileage to be earned by each rail and the prerogatives of rank of seniority. Mileage may be viewed as the distributive element of the basic economic good, collectively and exclusively controlled by various operating crafts organized into trade unions, such as the BLE, on a particular railroad district. The carrier owns the means of production, but the workers collectively control access of labor to production, in agreement with the carrier and in accordance with state and federal law.

One of the most common practices of a "sharpshooter" is done when working the extra board, which is a large rotating list of men protecting extra, vacated, and other unfilled assignments (as when a man is ill, on vacation, or marked off for rest). After studying the order of assignments of the extra board for the following day or so, the "sharpie" marks off the extra board for rest so that he misses an undesired run (a poor-paying night switch locomotive in a busy yard) and marks up for work so that he receives a preferred run (a high-paying through freight). Also, a sharpie may not claim a few earned minutes or may "steal" a few extra minutes so that he will return to the extra board in an advantageous position. Or a hoghead may sharpshoot on the job by killing time (for example, by pumping up the air on a cut of cars at a slower rate than ordinary) so that his yard locomotive ties up at the roundhouse after others on his shift, thereby causing him to miss a number of undesirable yard jobs. A large number of other strategies exist in sharpshooting, including the blatant act of registering less than one's cumulative mileage. By so doing a rail might make an extra round trip from Urbana to Crofts because he was ten miles under his maximum mileage for the month.

Reactions by rails against those endangering the good of mileage and of seniority generally vary according to the act threatening the welfare of the group. A sharpie caught not registering all of his earned miles receives, among other things, formal sanctions from the trade union, consisting of a restriction on the number of miles to be earned. Accordingly, at times, good acquired from sharpshooting is confiscated and returned to the collective pool of mileage to be earned by all. Other formal union sanctions include various local work rules obviating particular kinds of more readily controllable sharp practice. Informal reaction may be an individual or group act, for example, ridiculing a rail who "forgets" to register his miles or outmaneuvering a rail attempting to sharpshoot and thus thwarting his plan.

Individual and group informal sanctions may be in the form of jestful reprimand. Still stronger reprimand ranges along a continuum through intensities of derision to ostracism of the guilty party by other rails on and off the job. Derision of the stronger forms usually involves characterizations and is especially applied to repeated and blatant sharpshooters and to other etiquette-breaking behaviors. These behaviors spawn labels such as "scabby," "wormy," or "stoolie" (respectively, a rail who crosses a railroad picket line, one who is overly eager to switch more cars at faster speeds, and a rail who is guilty of informing company officers of infractions of operating rules or malingering on the job). The highly derogatory characterizations given to many good-threatening acts, for example the three just described, do "hurt" physically and undermine occupational status in the closed rail world. Sanctionative labels are used with a person's name as terms of address and reference ("Scabby Smith"), are seen chalked on the sides of rolling stock, and are heard long after a person's departure from the rail world. Once a severe label of sanction is applied to a rail it acts as a weapon to be unleashed by any rail at any time, under the most unanticipated of circumstances. A stigmatized rail cannot make an error on the job without having others comment upon it in an unsympathetic way. "What would you expect from a wormy bastard like Warden?"

An important informal group sanction against sharpshooting and other good-endangering behavior is known as "sandhouse gossip," or "sandhousing." When directed at transgressors against the code of rail etiquette, the gossip serves to unnerve the transgressor or the potential code breaker. Such gossip may also be on other subjects such as railroad current events and the personal situation of some rails. Sandhousing need not take place in the vicinity of the sandhouse (where locomotives are waiting to take on sand). It can happen anywhere—in a cab, caboose, switchtender's shanty, or bar—and can become increasingly malicious to fit the degree of flagrant abuse of norms of the craft group. "We 'take care' of our own," Timmy Gardner once said, concerning the control of behavior deviating from group norms.

OFF THE JOB

After inspecting what several other hogheads had accumulated in the way of miles, Slim turned away from the mileage register. He looked at the large bulletin board on the wall opposite the standard clock by which rails set their watches and over the table holding the bulletin books of carrier regulations and notices. On the bulletin board were various announcements concerning the health insurance provided by the carrier, the latest changes in the Railroad Retirement benefits, and information from the employees' credit union, golf club, and other voluntary associations, including a popular association for leisure activity of senior employees sponsored by the company. Two new notices attracted Slim's attention. One was a sign-up sheet for contributions to a switchman who had been severly injured in an automobile accident and was having trouble making ends meet financially. Slim signed the sheet and wrote "$10.00" after his name, as Timmy had done a short while before.

A second notice said that local Division Number 983 of the BLE had provided the funds, as was customary, for the wreath for Brother Jeb B. Newkirk, an engineer who had just died after a brief illness. The time and place of the funeral were given and Slim copied the information so that he could be present, provided that he was not called on duty—as was the case for the past three funerals he had tried to attend. The company always had first call on his time. As customary, a broken hand brake wheel was to be the design of the funeral wreath, an old design unique to railroaders. Rails on the CC & U do not remember its symbolism, but in the last century it was connected to a tale of the death of a brakeman. His remains were found with a wrecked freight car that he was hand braking to a stop. In his hands was found the broken hand wheel of the car's staff brake.

Getting into his auto in the darkness of night, Slim watched a switch locomotive shove ten new boxcars back toward a track full of cars. A switchman, visible only as a bobbing lantern, darted to the first car of the track of cars, undoubtedly to open the knuckle on the end of the automatic coupler, and darted out again in time to give his "easy" signal with his lantern. Coming back to Slim's mind was an incident in Crofts Yard at 3:00 A.M. on a dark and dusty night not long ago. In a situation similar to this, a long cut of cars was being backed against a track full of cars. Conductor Hearn and his brakeman were standing on the track and were hit by the moving cars. The brakeman was injured and Hearn was knocked onto the track and cut in half by the flanged steel wheels of the cars rolling over the steel rails. Within the hour Mrs. Hearn was awakened from her sleep in Urbana by a telephone call from a company representative. Not quite awake, she was told her husband had just been killed in Crofts. She came fully awake with the cold shock of the message. Slim was angry when, at Hearn's funeral, he learned of the abrupt predawn telephone message.

As Slim drove toward home down the dark nearly deserted streets, he reflected that he would get to see his wife and children before they went to bed. Many rail wives say they are forced to raise their children by themselves as their husbands sleep most of the day while working a regular assignment which reports to work between 10:30 P.M. and 1:00 A.M. Faith Lewis once related to Slim that many of the people in her church thought she was a widow. But, what really bothered her, she confided, were all of the noises in her house at night when her husband was out on a run. Jane Knarr told Slim and his wife that she and her husband, George, had had a three-day honeymoon in Urbana. That was all the time the company gave him off during a particularly busy period, and George had to call in each of the three days to see if he would be required to mark up on the extra board, which did not have enough men to protect all open assignments. "We went nowhere on a somewhat tension-ridden honeymoon," Jane said, in a matter-of-fact tone of voice. Jane learned early in her marriage that men working the extra board or in a freight pool can never leave the sound of the telephone. Indeed, the average railroader's family consists of a husband, a wife, several children, and a telephone.

In survey research on groups A, B, and C, working on the extra board is generally acknowledged to be a difficult job. The statement, "Everything considered, I think working the extra board is an easy job" evoked exceedingly negative responses averaging on a scale of 1 (strongly agree) through 5 (strongly disagree) as follows:

Group A	Group B	Group C
4.51	4.44	4.73

Almost as strong a response of this kind was given to the statement, "The demands of engine service, particularly demands of time of day on and off duty, length of time away from home, and being 'on call,' have had little or no negative effect upon my family and other personal life," as follows:

Group A	Group B	Group C
4.38	4.27	4.05

Engineer snags his orders on the Santa Fe on a lazy Sunday afternoon when most people are relaxing.

It would be good to get some sleep tonight without having to anticipate a telephone call before he woke up the next morning, Slim thought, as he pulled into his driveway. Many a night he would be in bed but not be able to sleep because he was expecting the crew dispatcher to call him on the telephone. He might be either "first or second out" for a call knowing that the train dispatcher definitely had to call at least two freight trains before dawn. A slight tension would prevent him from falling into a sound sleep. Some rails had his problem, and others did not. Many a time he would stay up for the eleven o'clock news on television and get only an hour's sleep or so, because he thought he would get out after dawn, but, instead, would be called for a run leaving at 2:30 A.M. On the other hand, sometimes he would stay by the telephone for more than six hours, "first out" waiting to be called for an eastbound drag of empties, but the roundhouse could not spare the units and the drag would not be called by the dispatcher. (The yardmaster could store his mile-long cut of empties on the second of the paired main lines running by the yard.) In another two hours he would be called for a regular eastbound freight. If he missed a call, he was subject to company discipline, and he would also go to the bottom of the working list where he could wait from one and one-half to three days until he was again "first out" and eligible to receive a call. Furthermore, if he missed a call, he could easily be short on his monthly mileage.

Entering his house, Slim was pounced upon by his two sons. The oldest would be the starting pitcher in a baseball game the day after tomorrow. Would Dad be there in the stands? As usual, the hoghead promised nothing but said he would have to see how close he would be to his call, if he were not already on the road. Related thoughts flowed through his mind—it was growing late; he would have little time remaining to chat with his sons before they went to bed; perhaps he would have no time for the ball game so important to the boys; regrettably, he had already missed his oldest son's graduation from junior high; maybe he would be able to make it for the graduation of the younger one. The only thing Slim could depend on was attending his own funeral, as he was once told by an old hoghead at the top of the seniority list. "Then you'll have all the time in the world, Sonny," the old head remarked.

8/Future trends for the hoghead

Ethnological study often suffers from what might be called "the isolation fallacy." Tribal peoples are studied and written about as if they existed in isolation from other tribal peoples and from societies with more advanced technologies. Interspecific patterns of culture shared between two neighboring tribal societies are not reported upon. The massive presence of alien culture contact may not be mentioned. Similarly, ethnologists study and report upon peasant communities as if they existed in isolation from the encompassing agrarian state, even though they know that theoretically this is a condition that cannot be. In this vein, many ethnologists say that we customarily study both primitive/tribal and peasant societies, despite the fact that no peasant group can exist apart from the state.

Ethnological study of communities and groups in contemporary United States and Canada often treats the subjects of research as though they were "isolated tribalists." Following the ethnological precedent set by W. Lloyd Warner and others (1967), the broader industrial societal setting of the group/community study of this book is considered and related to the presentation. In this chapter, we consider railroaders in terms of a developed country and then we review two customary ethnological concerns, demographics and sex roles of the subjects of research. The energetic bases of societal organization and development have been used by some ethnologists as the means of understanding tribal and agrarian groups. In this chapter, we use these energy bases as a frame for considerations of future conditions in American railroading. Accounts of technological innovation (or lack of it) and political and economic forces affecting railroading round out the placement of the hoghead in his greater societal setting. With this broader, "Warnerian" ethnological perspective, the rail world of the hoghead is made more meaningful to the reader and is tied to the relevancy of contemporary social issues and public policy. Some of the most valuable writings in the social science of industry are those where a case study relates to a larger societal perspective. In such writings an attempt is made to link the world of work to aspects of the wider social setting (Roth, Ryzek, and Daniels 1973:324).

RAILROAD GROWTH IN A DEVELOPED COUNTRY

The craft of the locomotive engineer generally prospers in relation to the well-being of American railroads, except that as the carriers invest in increased automation and in more efficient machines, less railroaders, including engineers, are employed. In order to consider the future of the hoghead, the future of business for the carriers in the economically developed countries of the United States and Canada, must be discussed. The discussion starts with a brief overview of the growth of American railroads. Historically viewed, the railroads have gradually been losing their share of the market of their bread and butter—the transportation of freight. In the United States the rail carriers had a comfortable 77.1 percent of the total freight traffic in 1929, 67.7 percent in 1939, 47.2 percent in 1950, 44.1 percent in 1960, 39.8 percent in 1970, and an estimated 36.7 percent in 1976. During this same period from 1929 to 1976, common carrier truck traffic increased from 3.3 to 22.6 percent, river and canal traffic from 1.4 to 11.6 percent, and pipeline traffic from 4.4 to 24.2 percent (source, AAR 1977a:36). Unregulated, noncommon carrier trucks increased their traffic in a manner similar to the truck lines, but their freight haulage is not included in the total freight from which the above percentages are calculated.

Over this span of almost fifty years, rail freight has increased in absolute tonnage. From 1929 through 1973 revenue freight traffic, measured in ton-miles or the product of the lading tonnage and the distance transported, nearly doubled from 447,322,000 to 851,809,000 (AAR 1977a:29). Although railroad percentages of freight business will probably continue to decline, the carriers should see a trillion ton-miles of freight before the end of this century. Put in perspective, since 1947, the beginning of our long sustained period of postwar economic growth, rail ton-miles increased only 30 percent despite a 175 percent increase in gross national product. The statistical trends given above for the United States also hold for Canada.

A recent, sometimes internally contradictory, study of the Department of Transportation (DOT) predicts (hopes?) that by 1990 freight ton-mileage for all modes of transportation will double in the United States and that the railroad share will be up to 42 percent. According to the DOT, a very large part of the growth in railroad ton-miles would be in the form of coal haulage from northwestern and northcentral states (AAR 1977b:3, 10–11). Indeed, in 1977 President Carter called for doubling 1974 coal production by 1985, and the railroads haul about two-thirds of all coal produced. This should augur well for an increase in rail ton-miles. However, demand for and production of coal has not yet shown any signs of spurting ahead to facilitate the presidential goal. Consequently, rail ton-miles could continue to grow only modestly as the rail percentage of total domestic freight ton-miles continues to slip or, at best, stabilizes. Stability of coal production is a factor upon which the political power of a president of the United States apparently has little effect. Thus production well may not double by 1985. Costly, ever-changing federal regulations on burning coal are well-intended, but also counter-productive to federal Energy Department attempts to promote use of coal.

One potential threat to railroad coal traffic is the coal slurry pipeline. Here coal is transported in pulverized form in a medium of vast amounts of water pumped through a special pipeline. Electrical generating firms see slurry lines as a means of combatting the constantly escalating rates of railroads for transportation of coal. Slurry lines have a significant long-term advantage in pricing over other modes of transport. Their major operating cost is servicing interest on their costs of construction. The interest cost is virtually immune to inflation. Rail lines, with about one-half of their revenue dollars going to labor costs, are highly inflation-prone in the pricing of their service (cf.Cook 1978). However, generally very high, but not completely known, capital costs of long pipelines and the problems of contamination of slurry water by coal, not to mention shortage of water, make the slurry line somewhat problematic for any long-distance use.

Another threat to rail transport of coal is the developing technology for generation of electricity in a power plant at the site of a coal mine. Pipelines and electrical transmission lines, unlike railroads and many truck lines, are not all-encompassing common carriers. Only such common carriers are obliged by law to haul virtually anything the public presents to them. Financial stability of rail carriers could be destroyed by pipe and electrical lines, which deprive railroads of their all-important coal traffic, thereby endangering public service by these common carriers.

A threat of another kind to growth of rail traffic is the developing possibility of governmental control of the routes, kinds, and speeds of potentially dangerous rail cargoes. In 1977 the carriers reported almost 8000 derailments. (Not all derailments are reported by local carrier officers to system officers.) Tank car accidents involving explosive and lethally caustic chemicals such as liquefied vinyl chloride, anhydrous ammonia, and propane are common. Detonation of boxcar loads of explosives are not unknown. Rail freight can be dangerous freight, destroying or requiring the evacuation of a town along a rail route. According to the accident reports of the National Transportation Safety Board, since 1969 major wrecks of tank cars have resulted in a disaster about once every six months. In these disasters, about fifty people have been killed, 1500 injured, and private and public property damaged in the amount of many tens of millions of dollars. Sometimes the tank cars, which are long cylinders having capacities ranging from 10,000 to 50,000 gallons, rocket away from the site of their derailment. In one accident a section of a burning tank car rocketed along, by the force of escaping compressed gas, for one-quarter mile and bounced off houses while it released flaming propane. Unless the carriers reduce the appreciable hazards to the public of dangerous freight, government regulations may slow, reroute, or shorten many trains to the point of great financial loss to the carriers. Unfortunately, part of the danger lies in the delapidated roadbed and rolling stock of many carriers, the correction of which is beyond their financial means.

Wrecking crane rights derailed chemical tank car on Houston Belt and Terminal in downtown Houston.

In 1929 the total number of railroad employees of all kinds was 1,660,850; by 1959 it had been cut to one-half (815,474) and by 1976 it had been cut to less then one-third (482,882) (AAR 1977a:57). Route mileage of railroads (not including sidings, spurs, and yard tracks) decreased from 249,433 in 1929 to 199,411 in 1975 (AAR 1977a:46) and will be decreased more as railroad routes are rationalized in the future (DOT 1977), thus further decreasing local freight and other jobs.

With climbing ton-mile productivity over time, through labor's use of more efficient machines such as modern diesels, radio, and CTC, railroaders handle and are responsible for increased amounts of freight tonnage. Railroaders decrease opportunities of railroad employment as they eliminate through their productivity many of the jobs they might wish to hold. The near demise of rail passenger service also contributed to the decrease of opportunities for varieties of railroad work. Because further opportunities exist for rationalization and automation in railroading, the number of railroaders including locomotive engineers should continue to decrease. It is possible, however, for the number to decrease only at a very modest rate, and for it almost to stabilize. Such stabilization of employment could come about in the long run because of limitations on energy resources in the industrial world and the consequently increased necessity for energy-efficient rail transport. More will be said on the subjects of energy and of railroad automation below.

RAIL DEMOGRAPHICS

Who will be numbered among the hogheads of the future? It looks as if young people will abound and women will definitely be part of the picture. Railroaders tend to be an older lot today. This is in part because of past socio-economic controls on the composition of the railroader population. During the Great Depression of the 1930s, virtually no railroaders were hired, and during the massive rail freight and passenger explosion of World War II, very many were employed. As railroad business expanded only slowly after the war, relatively few new employees were hired. Accordingly, masses of railroaders are scheduled to retire in the 1970s and early 1980s.

On the CC & U and its parent O & W system, about one-half of the present population of over 25,000 employees will retire in the next decade. About one-half of these employees were past fifty years of age in 1977. Many of those who "hired out" during World War II have been retiring throughout the 1970s. From 1971 to 1972 the average year of birth of locomotive engineers and firemen on survey railroad districts A, B, and C was, respectively, 1917, 1917, and 1915. (My nineteen-year-old research assistant thought at first that something was wrong with the computer programming of the data, but then he wrote across the computer printout: "These guys are old!")

As CC & U and other hogheads continue to retire at a marked rate over the next decade, more new apprentice engineers will make their seniority dates as locomotive firemen and will enter into formal training for the 150-year-old craft. Thus the public will see more and more "young runners," instead of the grizzled old heads still so common.

What will be noteworthy about the young runners is that they will be given formal instruction on the job, and in the classroom, workshop, and laboratory (locomotive simulator). For over a century, and until only a few years ago, firemen (hogheads in the making) were informally and sporadically instructed on the job according to the whims and varied abilities of the engineer on a particular run. Self-instruction from publications and annual or biannual examinations of operating and air brake rules provided supplements to the traditional learning by "osmosis." The dawn is now breaking on a new era of formally trained engineers seeking the long and varied experience of their older coworkers.

THE HOGHEAD IS A LADY

Perhaps more revolutionary than the developing change in the age of hogheads is the change concerning the sex of those in this occupation. Because of pressure from federal agencies, for the past few years the carriers have been hiring some women as engineer trainees. The women are well featured in carrier advertisements and in the media in public relations releases. Some women feel they are being exploited, but nevertheless seem to relish the personal attention given to them in the various media. To some extent, they *are* "show girls"; that is, hired in part to be shown to the public.

My experience and research led me to conclude long ago that a qualified woman would make just as good a hoghead as a qualified man. What qualified women need most to become a hoghead is development of a sense of self-esteem and confidence related to ultimate ability to perform well in the craft. Confidence building should be the most important part of the training of female engineers, if the carriers are truly interested in affirmative action in employment. Stress, for female firemen and engineers, often issues from not knowing what is expected of them at work. Also, the mild hazing and verbal and practical examining of all "students" is increased for females, adding to the stress. Many of the men are curious about standards of performance for their female counterparts and they frequently test their performance. As the female rail gains experience and a knowledge of the range of variation of demands of work, her self-image and ease of interpersonal relations on the job grows.

Limitations of physical strength on the part of females may place some restrictions on them in some railroad crafts, for example, brakemen and switchmen, where hand brakes and heavy track switches can pose problems. But the locomotive engineer/fireman no more needs great physical strength today than does the airline pilot or the helmsman of a large ship. Aside from some limitations regarding physical strength, no men's crafts and women's crafts *per se* exist today on the railroads or elsewhere in American industry. Nevertheless, throughout the world, women are frequently barred from men's occupations because they are said to lack the necessary qualifications.

In survey research among enginemen on railroad districts A,B, and C, with results ranging from 1 (strongly agree), to 5 (strongly disagree), the statement "A qualified woman could, in time, be trained to become a competent locomotive engineer" brought this response:

Group A	Group B	Group C
2.88	2.76	3.03

In late 1977 the first of three "lady hogheads" working at Urbana for the past few years made her solo run, to Crofts and back. Many males were looking for something to criticize, and she knew it, but everything went well on the trip. Undoubtedly, attitudes of the enginemen toward women as competent engineers will become more positive as more such runs are made without mishap. A number of mishaps and serious accidents in the Urbana terminal area over the past few years on the part of female engineers (most of them were restricted to yard service) have elicited strong condemnation of the women by male rails—criticism that was far more severe than if Joe or Pete had wrecked a locomotive.

One astute hoghead, Janice Adams, said, regarding negative comments she had heard from some rails and their wives about female engineers, "No one was against women working with the men as waitresses [in company bean-eries], as chambermaids [in company dormitories], and as cleaning ladies [in various company buildings]. They should have no problem with us now continuing to work with the men, only in higher paying positions."

Occupational sex-typing will be prevalent in the United States and Canada for a long time, especially among the rails, who have been practitioners of and protectors of the prerogatives of a "man's job" for a century and a half. Deeply rooted tradition dies hard. Male or female stereotypes of occupational roles in railroading are reinforced because, until very recently, few women had entered the ranks of the operating and nonoperating crafts. (During World War II with the shortage of *manpower,* some women were hired as nonoperating employees, but this practice was not continued in postwar years.) All of the behavioral expectations for role performance in railroading are tied up on conscious and subconscious levels with popular images of men at work. After all, it is the "little lady" who stays at home and awaits the return of her "brave engineer" in American folk song and folklore. The last stanza of the well-known folk song "The Wreck of Old 97" is didactic in intent for it reaffirms for women their subordinate place in the rail world (Botkin and Harlow 1953:450):

> Now ladies, you must take warning.
>   From this time now on [learn]:
> Never speak harsh words to your true loving husband,
>   He may leave you and never return.

Although the image of the male as a great hunter, plowman, high priest, or powerful chief is common, no panhuman common denominator for female or male work exists except for the bearing and nursing of babies by women. What is considered proper work according to a sexual division of labor is not understandable in a solely biological frame of reference, but must be understood with regard to cultural tradition. For example, among the Hopi, men spin, weave, and make clothing for themselves and for women. Among the Navajo, neighbors of the Hopi, women do the weaving. For the Hopi house building and repair is largely women's work. In hoe-agricultural production (horticulture) of foodstuffs, women do most of the work in sub-Saharan Africa, but the reverse is true among the Pueblo Indians of the American southwest. The shock troops of the large standing army of the formidible African kingdom of Dahomey consisted of 2500 female soldiers—amazons who lived apart from men. In the Soviet Union today, a majority of physicians and many locomotive engineers are women. What seems "natural" women's work in one time and place is not necessarily the same in another, for "natural" is culturally defined.

In railroading a woman gets equal pay for equal work without equivocation, and opportunity for promotion in the railroad crafts is automatic according to seniority. Although not yet accepted by her peers, the lady hoghead is here to stay. Brother Rogers and Brother Johnson will have to move over a bit on the bench in the register room and make a place for "Sister" Adams.

An experienced locomotive engineer, who has a degree in psychology.

ENERGETIC LIMITS TO GROWTH

In these days of increasing public concern about the ecology of industry and the energetic limits to growth of our industrial society, it is surprising that the railroad industry has not made a bigger positive impact upon the consciousness of Americans and Canadians. A railroad is truly an energy-efficient mode of transportation. Movement of highway freight and airway freight takes respectively almost four times and about sixteen times the energy as railway freight. Railway and waterway freight are about equally as energy efficient per ton-mile. However, because of the circuitous nature of many water routes, along channels not running directly from city A to city B, mileage of water carriers exceeds in many instances that of rail carriers. Theoretical efficiency of rail over truck carrier is limited somewhat by greater circuity of a rail route compared to that of a truck route between two cities. Railroads consume only about 7/10s of one percent of our national energy budget as compared to about 24 percent used by all other forms of transport, including the automobile.

Until it increased in 1979, the world price of petroleum was stable since it quintupled during 1973–1974. If the domestic price is significantly increased over a modest span of time, say doubled in the next ten years in addition to the cost effect of continued inflation, then the United States will need additional energy-efficient rail transport. It cannot begin to afford to do otherwise to maintain the American way of life, from standard of living to form of government. In future circumstances of doubled petroleum prices, railroads and rail employment would increase, and rail ton-miles could easily climb to 50 percent of the total freight hauled.

Ineffective public relations on the part of the industry is part of the answer to why the railroad has not made a bigger impact on the public consciousness. The railroad reinforces its image of being inept and a "loser" among industries by doing things like running a series of television commercials showing an astronaut wandering around some tracks while admonishing the audience that they need America's railroads. Yawn. The spaceman's exhortations were not substantiated in the commercials and railroading was not much in evidence in any event. "Johnny Cash gives more [audience-holding] information in one railroad song on his television shows than the [entire series of] T.V. commercials did," said hoghead John Lynd to a register room full of agreeing rails at Urbana Yard. By their own admission, American railroads are beset with very serious problems here on earth, thus the public found that the attempted projection of a space-age image lacked credibility and was strictly Madison Avenue. It was even rather ludicrous to some viewers.

The railroads are able to produce convincing educational advertisements if they so desire, such as a series they ran in *Railway Age* (May 27, 1974:37–40), which is read by an audience of railroad managers. The series explained in a straightforward fashion the inherent energy efficiencies of rail transport. The following six paragraphs builds upon the series in *Railway Age,* containing information that is common knowledge to most rails.

Steel wheels on steel rails offer less friction and resistance than any other element of contact on surface transportation vehicles. (Much greater friction is found in rubber tires on highways or in barge hulls on waterways.) Flanged steel wheels are self-guided on a track's paired rails, which are elevated up out of much of the results of inclement weather, such as ice and water. Guided movement of machines on rails of various kinds is the essential component of automation in many industries. Railways have had this potential for increasing automation for over fifteen decades.

A locomotive has a diesel engine with up to 20 cylinders, each having a volume of about 570 cubic inches. Much less fuel-consuming friction is present in the wall of a large cylinder of the rail diesel than in the greater number of small cylinders of the truck engines necessary to equal the hauling power of the diesel.

Air resistance of rail freight and passenger vehicles is minimal because rail cars draft one another. The locomotive cuts a "hole" through the resistance of the atmosphere and the cars follow in the "windbreak" created by its movement. A driver of a racing car uses a similar windbreak of low air pressure, when he gets on the tail of a leader and engages in "drafting," reducing the air resistance on the front of his racer. Railroad drafting offers an economy of great scale. At times a hoghead drafts 200 or more trailing cars along his guided way of rails.

One large rail diesel is cheaper to manufacture and maintain than the dozen or so smaller truck engines it would take to equal it in hauling power. On the level roadbed of the O & W system north of Central City, one 1500 h.p. diesel-electric unit (a six-axle type built 25 years ago) can pull 3100 trailing tons. Five brand-new 300 h.p. trucks can haul only a small fraction of that tonnage. Significant energy is used in building transport vehicles and their prime movers, or engines. Locomotives thus represent a savings in capital energy as well as maintenance and operating energy costs. Freight cars do not represent as large a savings because of low average freight car miles per day.

The number of crew members on a one-mile-long, 8000-ton freight train—presently, a hoghead, two brakemen, and a conductor—are far less than the number of truckers it would take to haul the same amount of freight. This statement, it should be added, takes into account the support needed for the freight train in the way of terminal crews on yard and industrial switchers.

Finally, existing rail roadways can easily handle double the ton-miles of today, and without paving over any additional land, as would be required to build more highways. Large amounts of energy are expended in construction and maintenance of highways and waterways, largely at public expense. It should be noted that freight trucks, because of their weight, require the construction of much heavier highways and highway bridges than would be the case for auto traffic alone. Trucks also break up highways at vastly greater rates than do autos. Construction and maintenance of truck-highways consume a significant amount of our national energy budget.

It should be added that the railroads consume about 20 percent of domestically burned diesel fuel, yet their locomotives produce less than one-half of one percent of the pollutants vented into the atmosphere. By truck, 1000 ton-miles produce 7.5 lbs. of exhaust-stack pollutants, and by rail only 2.1 lbs. are emitted (Hoffman 1974).

Electric locomotives give no direct atmospheric pollution on the 1200 route-miles of electrified American main line. But, the power plant that supplies the current to run the straight electric units does pollute to varying extents. Electric locomotives generally last longer than diesel-electrics, but the capital costs of installing electrification to a nonelectrified line is close to prohibitive for the capital-starved American carriers. The major benefit (largely a potential as yet) of electrification of railroads is that electrically propelled trains can use nonpetroleum sources of fuel, such as coal or nuclear energy, whereas trucks and aircraft cannot. The railroads, then, have a vast potential for freight and passenger hauling in a future where petroleum is very expensive or depleted. Studies are still under way on the feasibility of electrifying main lines with high traffic densities, but government subsidy may be the only route to selective rail electrification (cf. Anon. 1974a, 1974b, 1974c; Weiss 1976). To the extent that the United States is forced to change a significant part of its freight hauling from oil fuel to coal and nuclear fuel, railroad traffic and the need for "juice" hogheads (running electric locomotives) will increase.

Some time ago, on one western railroad the possibility of building nuclear-steam-electric locomotives was discussed. Besides the technical limitations inherent in reducing a shielded nuclear reactor to the 10-foot width of rail rolling stock, no more foolhardy of a combination could possibly be imagined. A nuclear power plant hurtling along at the head end of a fast heavy freight on the often rotten roadbeds of America's railroads would be more of a high-balling fright than highballing freight.

Not only will the climbing cost of fuel have an effect on the railroad share of freight ton-miles, but so will the eventual scarcity of fuel. Scarcity should increase cost, but cost is not the concern in the following. Recently recognized physical limits to our heretofore constantly expanding consumption of nonrenewable material resources, such as fossil fuels and metallic ores, but especially petroleum and natural gas, may take electric trains out from under the American Christmas tree and make them a full-scale reality. In the reality of a world up against material limits to economic growth, Americans would necessarily have to become more efficient in their industrial processes, or else suffer severe societal disequilibriums. The dawning recognition of physical limits to economic growth should lead to a greater use of rail freight and, in certain uses, rail passenger transportation because of inherent propulsion efficiencies (cf.Rice 1972). Less government capital for transportation would necessarily be allocated to government-developed and maintained highways, waterways, and airways (cf.AAR 1976) and more to privately owned (and government taxed) railways and pipelines.

Increasingly, it is recognized that railroads can effect significant energy savings in our economy. In a study of energy use in United States food systems, two scientists note that our total national food system, including production, processing, transport, and retailing, uses ever-increasing amounts of now quite expensive energy. Between 1940 and 1970 this increase was by about a factor of 3.2. The ever larger energy inputs into our food system boost food costs at home, and via exports, abroad, and consume greater amounts of our limited national energy budget. One important recommendation made by the two scientists with regard to beneficial energy reduction in our food system is that: "The trend toward the use of trucks in food transport, to the virtual exclusion of trains, should be reversed. By reducing the direct and indirect subsidies to trucks we might go a long way toward enabling trains to compete" (Steinhart and Steinhart 1974:315).

A new two-year study on energy, "The Workshop on Alternative Energy Strategies," states that the global oil supply will probably peak "around 1990 at the latest" (Flower 1978:42). The major conclusion of the study, with regard to petroleum, is highly significant for the future of railroads (Flower 1978:48):

> For governments and consumers to allow oil consumption to increase in the fond hope that more oil will somehow turn up is to run the risk that the complex interactions of geology, politics, economic growth and prices will instead dictate a drop in oil production even earlier than we have thought likely, thus increasing the difficulty of adjusting to a world in which oil is scarce.

Whether or not this jeremiad is heeded, the railroads could well experience a rebirth based upon their efficient use of energy.

TECHNOLOGICAL DEVELOPMENT

Already discussed have been the automated efficiencies of centralized traffic control and automatic train control on heavily used lines and the increasing hauling capacity of diesel-electric and straight electric units. All of these technologies will continue to evolve, thereby increasing the productivity of railroaders by means of their working with management's improving capital equipment. What else lies ahead for the hoghead?

The largest experiment to date with a fully automated freight train, where technology—specifically an in-cab computer—replaces the hoghead has recently failed (Anon. 1975). The latest state-of-the-art in railroad space-age technology could not run the one coal train for which a 78 route-mile, $54,000,000 railroad was built. Applications of nineteenth-century railroad technology were necessary to save the railroad of the twenty-first century. Instead of being automated, the three specially designed electric units, operating in multiple, needed not the ordinary engine crew of one, but two hogheads, and an electrician also, to insure operation of the "automatic" train, whose whistle also blew automatically, even at beer cans along the right of way. The "Beer Can Special" was a failure, but improved versions are just over the horizon (Corns 1979; Kalra 1979). Steam locomotives of the period 1800–1830 did not work too well either, and in one test a horse-drawn train beat the one pulled by the iron horse. Engineers can expect to have increased surveillance of their work in the cab by electronic devices which insure their alertness and compliance with some of the more basic operating and air brake rules. However, even a completely automated train of the future would need one engineer-overseer for reasons of safety.

The "automatic" coupler for railroad rolling stock is not automatic and is of a basic design dating into the last century, with all of the limited technological efficiencies of that cheap-labor-intensive period. In a similar manner, hoses for the air brake system must be coupled by hand between each piece of rolling stock. In the not too distant future, the hoghead should see the advent of a truly automatic coupler incorporating connections for the air brake line (in the manner of those used decades ago on electric, interurban rail cars). Locomotive couplers will have the capability of being operated from the cab, for the purpose of aligning and opening its knuckle.

Recently the railroads decided to scrap the Automated Car Identification System (ACI), widely applied in the past decade and *designed* to locate instantly any car on any American railroad. The ACI System uses horizontal layers of colored stripes to make a color-coded label on each car, identifying it according to its number. Trackside scanners relay car numbers to a central computer. The carriers contend that the ACI labels were not being read properly by the scanners, but the Federal Railroad Administration says that scanners would operate properly if the labels were kept clean. Carriers have spent $200,000,000 on ACI. Its abandonment amounts to a giant step backward in customer service and in the railroads' space-age technology, and a return to the days of a switch locomotive running up and down yard tracks and industrial spurs looking for a "lost" car. Perhaps the carriers do need some astronauts in space suits, but in this case equipped with buckets of hot soapy water and wiping rags. In any event, a major labor-saving device has been "deautomated."

Increasingly, the railroads are hauling highway trailer-on-flat-cars (TOFC), and metal containers similar to a trailer body (COFC). Trailers are of the same kind hauled across the country by truck drivers. Over the past two decades TOFC and COFC loadings have grown by a factor of six and are still waxing. Trailers, which should never have been introduced in the first place by the short-sighted carriers, will increasingly be replaced by containers. These can be loaded onto a ship or barge, stacked and stored empty or full, or temporarily placed on a relatively expensive truck-trailer chassis complete with running gear and license plates. Container trains have less weight, less wind resistance, and a lower center of gravity, and can use cheaper flat cars than trailer trains hauling the same freight tonnage. Most important, a container does not permanently tie up the capital of a truck chassis and does not require expensive license plates as the trailer does. Especially vital in the growth of COFC is the "landbridge" (or "railbridge") traffic in which marine containers are moved on one bill-of-lading from one terminal to another by combined rail and ocean transportation. Today, much containerized freight moves from Europe to the Orient and vice versa via trans-Pacific and trans-Atlantic ships and across North America by train. The necessity of the Panama Canal for virtually all merchandise cargo has been eliminated. A transcontinental railbridge route is almost 3,000 miles shorter than a coast-to-coast route through the Panama Canal, and it provides a significant savings in fuel for transportation. Most TOFC/COFC traffic represents cargo formerly hauled in boxcars—railbridge freight is a clear exception.

Inevitably, greater use of COFC/TOFC means less jobs for rails. As a freight train enters a long track straddled by a giant unloading crane at its terminal yard, it is quickly unloaded by a crane operator and reloaded by him later on. Yard switch and industrial switch locomotives and their crews are not needed for the one-hundred or more loads brought by the train. A truck driver takes each trailer or container to its unloading site. Multiply this practice by several such trains in each direction on each main line in the United States and Canada and large numbers of jobs are eliminated, even more so as COFC/TOFC continues to grow. Generally, evolving railroad technology such as TOFC/COFC eliminates jobs, but it will not eliminate the need for an engineer on remaining trains.

It is noteworthy that the federal government ships a considerable part of the United States mail, once carried largely by passenger trains in special "head end" cars, via TOFC/COFC in freight trains instead of on its own Amtrak passenger trains. These desperately need the nonpassenger revenue to reduce operating deficits. TOFC/COFC transportation of mail on Amtrak passenger trains could result in stable rail passenger service for the United States and more jobs in this service. But, then, no one has ever accused the federal government of having a rational policy for transportation, as we shall see.

DIVERSIFICATION, NATIONALIZATION, AND REGULATION

Of the problems in business organization clouding the future of the hoghead and other rails, one that is well-developed is diversification of railroads. Other significant problems are nationalization and regulation. Many carriers such as the O & W of which the CC & U is a part, are diversifying their assets into nonrailroad business ventures: real estate, petroleum and mining, and services and manufacturing. Part of the thought behind such diversification is the need for earnings from nonrailroad business, which are almost all more profitable than the meager earnings of railroad companies. The nonrailroad earnings are generated allegedly to strengthen and protect the diversified carrier and to lessen its economic vulnerability to the ups and downs of the business cycle. What has actually happened is that more and more railroads are not just diversifying but are becoming conglomerate corporations—holding companies, often called "industries," in which the railroad is not the nourished parent but the nourishing stepchild feeding the growth of the more profitable and glamorous diversified businesses (cf.Myers 1974; ICC 1977).

Assets of the diversifying railroad are often pumped into the holding company to the detriment of the carrier. One of the largest railroads in the country went bankrupt in part because of such practice. Four railroads have been "spun-off," that is sold by the holding company which was created with their assets—land, securities, cash, and credit. Even though some present-day managers of a holding company are favorably disposed to its underlying railroad, no guarantee exists that the next generation of managers will not find the railroad an economic drag to be eliminated in a financially advantageous business arrangement.

The danger to the future of private-enterprise railroading is that instead of investing capital in new rolling stock and track, railroad assets are being used by the holding company to purchase fast-food firms and the like. Pouring railroad cash into a chain of Speedy Taco stands does not help get the trains over the road. And not all of the glamorous diversifications have paid off. Some have been bad, money-losing investments. As a noted investment newsletter explained, a nonrail subsidiary of the O & W suffered a massive write-off of many tens of millions of dollars because of zero returns on an investment involving risk.

It is now too late for government to legislate against diversification of railroads by means of holding companies. Today, significantly more than one-half of rail ton-miles are moved by conglomerate holding companies and not by railroad companies. In any event, the carriers, under our free enterprise system, are free to do anything that is legal with their assets, including diversification and even disinvestment, by eventually spinning off the railroad from the conglomerate. In our economic system railroads are supposed to be profit-making firms protecting the interests of the investor-stockholders; they are not like government-owned firms, dedicated in part to rendering public service as, for example, are European railroads. In any case, little good for a railroad transportation firm seems ultimately to come from diversification, as one railroad analyst notes (Myers 1974:69):

> The claim is often made that diversification with its attendant holding company is an aid to railroads. This appears largely false. In the various examples studied and reported by the ICC, no clear case is visible where the diversification helped a railroad.

Many American railroads are no longer profit-making firms, and for that reason a large part of our route mileage is that of bankrupt carriers. Average railroad return on net investment was about 1 percent in 1977 and 1978 and the return has not exceeded 3 percent since 1966 (AAR 1977a:20). Only one major railroad in the entire world outside the United States (in Canada) is a privately owned carrier. All the rest are nationalized. Some critics of railroad management in America, including critics who are in railroad labor, have long advocated nationalization; that is, ownership and operation by the central government. Almost all American through-passenger service and the freight and local passenger service on much of the route mileage in the northeast and midwest are controlled today by government corporations. These, through circumlocutions and much involved explanation, are said not to be nationalized railroad carriers, perhaps because that is a dirty word in our nominally free-enterprise system. The corporations look and act like nationalized railroads, but are called something else. It is alleged that they will someday operate at an economic profit. One thing is certain about nationalized railroads by any name: They would not have their futures sold short by diversification and possible disinvestment.

On the subject of nationalization of railroads in general and of passenger service in particular, engine service employees on districts A,B, and C ranged from almost neutral through moderately negative. The statement, "The Federal government should own and operate railroads" was answered most positively by the numerous men at Urbana and Jackson terminals (Group A) on a scale from 1 (strongly agree) to 5 (strongly disagree):

Group A	Group B	Group C
3.08	3.76	3.48

Regarding passenger trains, the men responded as follows to this question: "The Federal government should not completely own and operate the railroads, but only their passenger assets and service":

Group A	Group B	Group C
3.59	3.18	3.51

More men of Group A wanted general nationalization than that of passenger service only. Group C was consistent on both questions. Group B had very many passenger runs on their district; they probably thought these would be maintained more by government than private enterprise.

Ecologist Barry Commoner has added fresh insight and fuel to the argument for the nationalization of American railroads (1973). The crux of Commoner's argument, also maintained by the Association of American Railroads and by myself, is that the logic of ecology fosters one underlying thought about railroads—they are far more efficient than other modes of transport in moving freight and passengers at minimum cost to environment and to diminishing reserves of fuels. Thus we will necessarily have to rely more upon railroads as an answer to our growing energy and environmental problems. However, Commoner goes further with a second underlying thought (1973:86):

At the same time it is equally true that no railroad, anywhere in the world, has been able to provide all . . . services to society at a cost sufficiently competitive to support profitable operation. . . . If we give up the demand for profitable operation, which means that the railroads can become publicly owned, then they can be rebuilt to provide the country with environmentally clean, energetically thrifty transportation. The choice is between social and private profit.

The latest and strongest arguments against nationalization are those found in the fourth of a series of studies by one of best managed, and most profitable of America's carriers (Union Pacific 1977). Unfortunately, the comparison of operations of American railroads with selected foreign ones does not include those of the Soviet Union, which has massive movement of rail freight on a scale comparable to that of our country. The study notes that nationalized railroads lose money. (West German railroads lost more than $4 billion in 1975, and the Japanese railroads owe their government $14.6 billion in probably unrepayable loans.) Further, costs of transport per-ton-mile are greater for nationalized railroads than for those of private enterprise. Nationalized railroads do not guarantee a particular level of employment or amount of service, as most of these firms are cutting back on route-mileage, workers, and service. However, lack of comparison with the more comparable Soviet Union and the fact that the nationalized railroad of Canada hauls freight more inexpensively than the average American carrier discount to some extent the arguments against nationalization found in the study. European and Japanese railroads used as comparisons in the study have unprofitable, short freight hauls with lightweight rolling stock moved in short trains. (For more on Canadian nationalized railroading, see Stevens 1973.)

The report correctly notes that nationalization transfers cost of railroad operations from one sector of the economy (private) to another (public). Furthermore, in the public sector, decisions affecting railroad transportation of passengers and freight will be made for political (read "social") rather than economic reasons. Many critics of privately owned railroads would argue that the political aspect of economic decisions in railroading should be taken into account anyway. Otherwise, the public sector and the consumer must pick up part of the bill, for the social consequences of the allegedly purely economic actions (cf. Cottrell 1951). For example, economic dislocations may be caused among workers, or manufacturers, or farmers as a result of railroad rationalization of its operations, and society as a whole then has to pay for the dislocations in unemployment benefits, reduced taxes, and higher costs of food and factory-made goods. Finally, the report advocates the mending of "weak links" in the American freight system "with *temporary* financial aid from Government" (Union Pacific 1977:xvi). Critics would reply that no guarantee can be made by the carriers of the "temporary" nature of the financial aid, and thus that they ask for the benefits of nationalization without the obligations. After all, the loans of the Japanese government to the Japanese railroads are also "temporary." As one old rail said in Urbana Yard, "In this country it's socialism for the big companies and free enterprise for the little guy."

Government regulation of operations by common carriers of all kinds (what

Amtrak's Sunset Limited, *No. 1, being serviced at El Paso. What is the proportion of government subsidy to operating costs for Amtrak compared to that for buses and airlines using government highways and airways?*

they may and may not do and their obligations as common carriers to the public) considered in its broadest sense has always included modest amounts of economic subsidy. In 1976, according to the Association of American Railroads, federal, state, and local government spent $33 billion for intercity transportation systems and facilities. Expenditures were for highways ($28.1 billion), airways ($3.8 billion), waterways ($1.3 billion) and railways (AAR 1976a). The AAR does not present 1976 government expenditures for railroads in a summary way that is comparable to the figures for other modes of transport. The AAR allows the reader to infer that government expenditures are modest for nonbankrupt railroads carrying freight only. But, considering federal aid to Amtrak ($500,000,000 per annum) and to bankrupt carriers ($1,000,000,000 per annum to Conrail alone), and federal, state, and local aid to rail commuter service, the total is not as negligible as might be inferred from AAR presentations (cf. also Friedman 1978, 1979). Nevertheless, the railroads, investing in and paying taxes on their privately owned rights of way, are at a disadvantage in competition with carriers in other modes of transportation paying relatively light or no user charges for movement over publicly owned and maintained rights of way.

Secretary of Transportation Brock Adams is interested in correcting the inequities between government subsidies for the railroads and for other modes of transportation. The public was informed of the problem of inequities in an essay of his, designed for a nonspecialist audience (1975). He notes that the larger problem is one of lack of government coordination and overall planning for the regulating and subsidizing of all modes of transport. Government policies for each mode of transport grew piecemeal over the years, with no view of the interrelated effects for all transportation and for the welfare of the country. Many practices in transportation that are inefficient and waste resources are protected from the corrective action of the marketplace by governmental regulation that is misguided, out of date, or both. Clearly, the time is at hand for correction of government policy and for regulation of transportation industries. Such correction can only benefit the railroads.

With the permanence of the not yet fully recognized energetic limits to our economy and the beginning of an awareness of the need for rational change in public policy for all transportation, the future of American railroads appears secure. However, prematurely optimistic notes have been sounded in the past for the renaissance of the rail carriers (cf. Hungerford 1945; Anon. 1967; Barloon 1967). Space-age technology may never be applied to the railroads, but perhaps Automatic Car Identification will make a comeback so that cars will not be lost. And perhaps a truly automatic coupler will bring the technology of joining cars in trains into the twentieth century. Increasing industrial-age automation and electronic surveillance of the hoghead's on-the-job tasks will not lead to his or her elimination as a highly responsible operator on the head end of the train. The locomotive engineer will be a valued worker on the railroads of the twenty-first century, which may well be nationalized in order to be rationalized in accordance with the economic *and* social requirements of a changing American society.

The reader desiring additional information on many of the topics covered in *The Hoghead* should see the references cited at the end of this book. Especially valuable are AAR 1974, 1976b, 1976c, 1977c, and RRIS n.d., all of which are bibliographic sources concerning railroads. A recent comprehensive work on railroading is John Armstrong's *The Railroad,* 1978.

References

AAR (Association of American Railroads), 1965, *The Standard Code of Operating Rules*. Washington, D.C.: AAR Operations and Maintenance Department.

———, 1974, *Textbooks on Railroads*. Washington, D.C.: AAR Office of Information and Public Affairs.

———, 1976a, *Government and Private Expenditures for Highway, Waterway, Railroad, and Air Rights-of-Way*. Washington, D.C.: AAR Economics and Finance Department.

———, 1976b, *Railroad Film Directory*. Washington, D.C.: AAR Office of Information and Public Affairs.

———, 1976c, *A Bibliography of Railroad Literature*. Washington, D.C.: AAR Office of Information and Public Affairs.

———, 1977a, *Yearbook of Railroad Facts, 1977*. Washington, D.C.: AAR Economics and Finance Department.

———, 1977b, *A Synopsis of the Department of Transportation's* National Transportation Trends and Choices (To Year 2000). Washington, D.C.: AAR Office of Information and Public Affairs.

Aaron, Benjamin et al., 1977, *The Railway Labor Act at Fifty*. Washington, D.C.: National Mediation Board.

Adams, Brock, 1975, "The Shameful State of Transport," *Reader's Digest* (February): 1-6.

Adams, Charles Francis, Jr., 1879a, "The Automatic Electric Block System," *Railroad Gazette* 11:592–593.

———, 1879b, *Notes on Railroad Accidents*. New York: Putnam.

American Railway Association, 1893, *Proceedings of the General Time Convention and Its Successor the American Railway Association from Its Organization April 14, 1886 to October 11, 1893 Inclusive*. New York: American Railway Association.

Anon., 1903, "Surprise Checking of Locomotive Runners," *The Railroad Gazette* 35:447.

———, 1967, "Railroads: The Comeback Is Getting Up Steam," *Forbes* (January): 16-22.

———, 1974a, "Electrification Looking Increasingly Attractive to U.S. Railroads," *Railway Locomotives and Cars* (February): 12-14.

———, 1974b, "Government Will Have Major Role in Any U.S. Mainline Electrification," *Railway Age* (8 April): 31.

———, 1974c, "Could Electrification in U.S. Follow the European Pattern?" *Railway Locomotives and Cars* (June/July): 10-13.

———, 1975, "A Railroader's Bad Day at Black Mesa," *Business Week* (4 August): 69–70.

Armstrong, John H., 1978, *The Railroad—What It Is, What It Does: The Introduction to Railroading.* Omaha, NE: Simmons-Boardman.

Armstrong, John S., 1957, "All About Signals—I, II," *Trains,* 17(8):44–57; 17(9):44–54.

Ashton, T.S., 1969, *The Industrial Revolution 1760–1830.* London: Oxford University Press.

Bacon, Francis, 1960, *The New Organon,* F. H. Anderson, ed. New York: Liberal Arts Press [First Published in Latin in 1620].

Bass, Bernard M., and G. V. Barrett, 1972, *Man, Work, and Organizations: An Introduction to Industrial and Organizational Psychology.* Boston: Allyn and Bacon.

Barloon, Marvin J., 1967, "The Coming of the Super-Railroad," *Harper's* (April):63–68.

Beck, James H., ed., 1978, *Rail Talk: A Lexicon of Railroad Language.* Gretna, NE: James Publications.

Becker, Howard S., and Blanche Geer, 1957, "Participant Observation and Interviewing: A Comparison," *Human Organization,* 16(3): 28–32.

Beebe, Lucius, 1938, *High Iron.* New York. Appleton.

Blaine, David G., 1975, "The Importance of Being Able to Stop: The Westinghouse Air Brake Story—1," *Trains,* 35(12):44–53.

———, 1975, "Load-To-Tare Ratios vs. Braking: The Westinghouse Air Brake Story—2," *Trains,* 36(2):48–53.

———, 1976, "Post-Zephyr Braking: The Westinghouse Air Brake Story—3," *Trains,* 36(3):40–46.

Botkin, B.A., and Alvin F. Harlow, 1953, *A Treasury of Railroad Folklore.* New York: Bonanza Books.

Cook, James, 1978, "What's Yours Is Mine," *Forbes* (6 March):76–77.

Corns, John B., 1979, "Ohio's Robot Railroad," *Trains,* 39(5):22–28.

Cottrell, W. Fred, 1939, "Of Time and the Railroader," *American Sociological Review,* 4:190–198.

———, 1951, "Death by Dieselization: A Case Study in the Reaction to Technological Change," *American Sociological Review,* 16:358–365.

———, 1964, "Technology and Social Change on American Railroads." In G. K. Zollschan and W. Hirsch, eds., *Explorations in Social Change.* Boston: Houghton Mifflin.

———, 1970, *Technological Change and Labor in the Railroad Industry: A Comparative Study.* Lexington, MA: Heath Lexington Books.

Cottrell, W. F., and H. C. Montgomery, 1943, "A Glossary of Railroad Terms," *American Speech,* 3:161–169.

Commoner, Barry, 1973, "Trains into Flowers: An Argument for the Nationalization of American Railroads," *Harper's* (December):78–86.

Crosby, John R., 1978, "Featherbraining," *Trains,* 38(10):66.

Dalby, Harry A., 1904, *Train Rules and Train Dispatching.* New York: The Locomotive Publishing Company.

Devoe, D. B., 1974, "An Analysis of the Job of Railroad Train Dispatcher," *Technical Report FRA–ORD&D-74-37.* Federal Railroad Administration, DOT.

Devoe, Donald B., and Anne W. Story, 1973, "Guidelines for Writing Railroad Operating Rules," *Technical Report FRA-RT-74-1.* Federal Railroad Administration, DOT.

Diesel, Rudolf, 1894, *Theory and Construction of a Rational Heat Motor.* New York: Spon and Chemberlain.

DOT (Department of Transportation), 1977, *Final Standards, Classification, and Designation of Lines of Class I Railroads in the United States,* vols. 1 and 2. Washington, D.C.

Flower, Andrew R., 1978, "World Oil Production," *Scientific American,* 238(3): 42–49.

Fogel, R. W., 1964, *Railroads and American Economic Growth.* Baltimore: Johns Hopkins Press.

Forman, Harry W., 1904, *Rights of Trains on Single Track: A Complete Examination for Employes on the Standard Code and Other Recommended Train Rules.* New York: Railroad Gazette.

Friedman, Jesse J., 1978, *Federal Aid to Railroads.* Washington, D.C.: Water Transport Association.

———, 1979, *Federal Aid to Railroads: Part II.* Washington, D.C.: Water Transport Association.

Gamst, Frederick, C., 1969, *The Qemant: A Pagan-Hebraic Peasantry of Ethiopia.* New York: Holt, Rinehart and Winston.

———, 1974, *Peasants in Complex Society.* New York: Holt, Rinehart and Winston.

———, 1975a, "Human Factors Analysis of the Diesel-Electric Locomotive Cab." In D. H. Harris, ed., *Human Factors,* Special Issue on Civil Systems, 17:149–156.

———, 1975b, "Rethinking Leach's Structural Analysis of Color and Instructional Categories in Traffic Control Signals," *American Ethnologist,* 2:271–296.

———, 1975c, "The Diesel-Electric Locomotive as a Work Environment: A Study in Applied Anthropology, *Rice University Studies* (Studies in Cultural Anthropology), 61(2):37–78.

———, 1977, "An Integrating View of the Underlying Premises of an Industrial Ethnology in the United States and Canada," *Anthropological Quarterly* (Golden Anniversary Special Issue on Industrial Ethnology), 50 (1):1–8.

Gamst, Frederick, C., and Edward Norbeck, eds., 1976, *Ideas of Culture: Sources and Uses.* New York: Holt, Rinehart and Winston.

Hall, Richard H., 1975, *Occupations and the Social Structure,* 2d ed. Englewood Cliffs, N.J.: Prentice-Hall.

Harris, Marvin, 1971, *Culture, Man, and Nature: An Introduction to General Anthropology.* New York: Crowell.

Hilton, George W., 1976, "Slack," *Trains,* 36(4):22–28.

———, 1978, "What Does the ICC Cost You and Me?" *Trains,* 38(8):28–32.

Hoebel, E. Adamson, 1972, *Anthropology: The Study of Man.* New York: McGraw-Hill.

Horowitz, Morris A., 1960, *Manpower Utilization in the Railroad Industry: An Analysis of Working Rules and Practices.* Boston: Bureau of Business and Economic Research Northeastern University.

Hoffman, Jack G., 1974, "Energy/Environment Balance." *Railway Locomotives and Cars* (April/May):31; (June/July):34–35.

Hubbard, Freeman H., 1945, *Railroad Avenue: Great Stories and Legends of American Railroading.* New York: McGraw-Hill.

Hungerford, Edward, 1945, *A Railroad for Tomorrow.* Milwaukee: Kalmbach.

Industrial and Labor Relations Review, 1971, *Labor Relations in Transportation* (Special Issue) 25(1).

ICC (Interstate Commerce Commission), 1977, *Railroad Conglomerates and Other Corporate Structures.* Washington, D.C.: ICC.

Jacobs, Warren, 1939, "Early Rules and the Standard Code," *Railway and Locomotive Historical Society Bulletin,* 50:29–55.

Josserand, Peter, ed., 1945, *Rights of Trains, A Complete Analysis of Single Track Standard Code Rules, by the Late Harry W. Forman,* 5th ed. New York: Simmons-Boardman.

Kalra, Paul S., 1979, "A Green Light for Advanced Train Controls," *IEEE Spectrum* (February):44–49.

Kemnitzer, Luis S., 1973, "Language Learning and Socialization on the Railroad." *Urban Life and Culture,* 1:363–378.

———, 1977, "Another View of Time and the Railroader," *Anthropological Quarterly,* 50:25–29.

Kroeber, A. L., 1948, *Anthropology.* New York: Harcourt.

Lazar, Joseph, 1953, *Due Process on the Railroads.* Los Angeles: Institute of Industrial Relations, UCLA.

Lynd, Robert S., and H. M. Lynd, 1929, *Middletown.* New York: Harcourt.

McCord, Carey P., 1948, "Life and Death by the Minute," *Industrial Medicine,* 17:377–382.

Mater, Dan H., 1939, "Seniority Rights Before the Courts," *Journal of Business,* 12:152–174.

———, 1940–1941, "The Development and Operation of the Railroad Seniority System," *Journal of Business,* 13:387–419; 14:36–67.

———, 1941, "A Statistical Study of the Effects of Seniority Upon Employee Efficiency," *Journal of Business,* 14:169–204.

———, 1941, "Effects of Seniority System Upon the Welfare of the Employee, the Employer and Society," *Journal of Business,* 14:384–418.

Myers, Edward T., 1974, "The Great Railroad Robbery: Disinvestment," *Modern Railroads* (September):67–72.

NTSB (National Transportation Safety Board), 1971a, "Illinois Central Railroad Company Train No. 1 Collision with Gasoline Tank Truck . . . Loda, Ill. January 24, 1970," *Report No. NTSB-RHR-71-1.* Springfield, VA: U.S. Dept. of Commerce, NTIS.

———, 1971b, "Special Study: Signals and Operating Rules As Causal Factors in Train Accidents," *Report No. NTSB-RSS-71-3.* Springfield, VA: U.S. Dept. of Commerce, NTIS.

———, 1977a, "Union Pacific Railroad Freight Train Derailment, Hastings, Neb. August 2, 1976," *Report No. NTSB-RAR-77-1.* Springfield, VA: U.S. Dept. of Commerce, NTIS.

———, 1977b, "Collision of an Amtrak/Atchison, Topeka and Santa Fe Railway Train and a Tractor-Cargo Tank Semitrailer, Marland, Okla. December 15, 1976," *Report No. NTSB-RHR-77-3.* Springfield, VA: U.S. Dept. of Commerce, NTIS.

Pelto, Pertti J., 1970, *Anthropological Research: The Structure of Inquiry.* New York: Harper & Row.

Pilcher, William W., 1972, *The Portland Longshoremen: A Dispersed Urban Community.* New York: Holt, Rinehart and Winston.

Platonow, German Alexandrowitsch, 1971, *Mensch-Machine-Systeme in Eisenbahnwesen, Eine Ingenieurung Psychologische Betrachtung.* Berlin: Transpress VEB Verlag für Verkehrswesen {Translated from the original Russian by R. Bohndorf and H. Kullik}.

Radcliffe-Brown, A. R., 1935, "On the Concept of Function in Social Science," *American Anthropologist,* 37:394–402.

————, 1952, *Structure and Function in Primitive Society.* Glencoe, IL: Free Press.

Rehmus, Charles M., 1971, "Collective Bargaining and Technological Change on American Railroads." In H. M. Levinson, et al., *Collective Bargaining and Technological Change in American Transportation.* Evanston, IL: Transportation Center at Northwestern University, pp. 85–242.

Richardson, Reed C., 1963, *The Locomotive Engineer, 1863–1963:* A Century of Railway Labor Relations and Work Rules. Ann Arbor: Bureau of Industrial Relations, University of Michigan.

Rice, Richard A., 1972, "System Energy and Future Transportation," *Technology Review* (January):31–37.

Risher, Howard W., Jr., 1971, "The Negro in the Railroad Industry." In H. R. Northrop, et al., *Negro Employment in Land and Air Transport.* Philadelphia: Wharton School of Finance and Commerce, University of Pennsylvania, pp. i-202.

Roth, Julius A., S. K. Ruzek, and A. K. Daniels, 1973, "Current State of the Sociology of Occupations," *Sociological Quarterly,* 14:309–333.

RRIS (Railroad Research Information Service), *Railroad Research Bulletin.* Washington, D.C.: National Research Council, National Academy of Sciences.

Schneider, Eugene V., 1969, *Industrial Sociology: The Social Relations of Industry and the Community,* 2d ed. New York: McGraw-Hill.

Shaw, Robert B., 1978, *A History of Railroad Accidents, Safety Precautions and Operating Practices.* Northern Press.

Steinhart, John S., and Carol E. Steinhart, 1974, "Energy Use in the U.S. Food System," *Science* 184:307–316.

Stevens, G. R., 1973, *History of the Canadian National Railways.* New York: Macmillan.

TFRP (Task Force on Railroad Productivity), 1973, *Improving Railroad Productivity.* Washington, D.C.: The National Commission on Productivity and the Council of Economic Advisors.

Tway, Patricia, 1977, "Industrial Ethnology and Changing Conditions in the Work Environment," *Anthropological Quarterly,* 50:19–24.

Union Pacific Railroad Company, 1977, *A Survey of Railroads in Selected Industrial Countries.* New York.

Warner, W. L., D. B. Unwalla, and J. H. Trimm, eds., 1967, *The Emergent American Society,* vol. 1: "Large-Scale Organizations." New Haven: Yale University Press.

Weiss, Willard D., 1976, "Electrification: U.S. Dawdles While the Rest of the World Turns on," *Railway Age* (23 February):28–31.

Whishaw, Francis, 1842, *The Railways of Great Britain and Ireland Practically Described as Illustrated,* 2d ed. London: J. Weale.

Glossary

Words in *italics* are cross-references to other words in the glossary.

ABS: Automatic *block signal* system.

ATC: Automatic train control system. A system that automatically stops a train exceeding a predetermined speed with regard to signal indications and track restrictions, when engineer does not acknowledge ATC warning whistle and take action to control train properly. (In this book, includes ATS, Automatic Train Stop, a more limited version of ATC.)

ABSOLUTE SIGNAL: A *home* signal governing the movement of *trains* and superseding superiority of trains by other rules. May be *block* or *interlocking* signal.

AGREEMENT: Labor contract between a railroad (or former independent railroad) and a railroad labor union. Agreements for operating crafts may run about 250 pages each.

AIR MAN: An *engine service* employee with better than average skills in train handling.

ALIBI: Excuse for not performing properly on the job.

APE CAGE: Caboose. Also, buggy, crummy, hack, hearse, and parlor.

AUTOMATIC BRAKES: All of train (locomotive and cars) brake system applying brakes by *reduction* of brake pipe/train line pressure up to certain limits.

BARN: Roundhouse.

BAD ORDER: *Rolling stock* or appliance in need of repair.

BEANERY QUEEN: A waitress.

BEANS: A meal.

BIG HOLE: Emergency position of automatic brake valve and emergency application of *automatic brake* system.

BLIND SHOVING OR RUNNING: Not being able to see or to have someone in control see the route over which a movement rolls.

BLOCK: (1) A designated length of track, usually between consecutive *home* signals; (2) A cut of cars destined for the same place.

BLOCK SIGNAL: A fixed signal at the entrance to or within a *block* governing movement of trains. May be of three basic types: color light, semaphore (having an arm, or blade, in addition to a color light), or position light (where a sequence of lights generally duplicates the position of a semaphore arm).

BOOK OF RULES: Small format handbook of 200 to 350 pages containing operating rules, and sometimes safety rules and mechanical and air brake rules and train handling regulations.

BRAKE PIPE: The part of the air brake piping of a locomotive or car acting as a supply pipe for car air reservoirs and providing the communication (of air pressures) by which *automatic brakes* are controlled. Piping of each car or locomotive unit can be joined to that of another car or unit by means of an air hose at each end. Also, train line.

BROTHER: Fellow union member, of a brotherhood.

BROWNIES: Demerits placed on a personnel record for rules infractions.

BULL: Railroad policeman. Also, cinder dick and gum shoe.

BUMP, TO: To displace a person with less seniority from his or her assignment by taking it, in accordance with the *agreement* of a particular craft.

CAB: Control compartment of a locomotive, containing engineer's workspace on its right-hand side.

CAR KNOCKER: Carman who inspects and repairs cars. Also, car toad and car whacker.

CENTRALIZED TRAFFIC CONTROL (CTC): Operations in which *trains* are moved over designated districts by wayside signal indications, which are controlled by a train dispatcher or other employee from a centrally located control panel. CTC usually also remotely controls important main line track switches. Wayside signals are *block* or *interlocking signals.*

CLEARANCE: (1) A form issued by the train dispatcher authorizing movement of a train between certain stations and containing other information; (2) Space between top and sides of *rolling stock* and structures along right of way such as bridges, tunnels, and parallel track containing rolling stock.

COMPANY, THE: A railroad employees' designation of the railroad of employment.

COUPLER: Massive and heavy steel jaws at each end of every piece of *rolling stock* used to attach these together.

CUT, OF CARS: Two or more cars coupled.

DARK TRACK/TERRITORY: A railroad district not having wayside *block* or *interlocking* signals for spacing of trains.

DELAYER: Train dispatcher.

DERAIL: A rail-inserted or mounted protective device which prevents rolling stock from rolling past a particular spot on the track, by throwing it off the rails.

DEADHEAD: (1) Employee traveling by means of a train pass on company business. Also done by automotive vehicle; (2) Rolling stock being moved from one station to another while not in revenue service.

DIE, TO: Circumstance in which crew is "dead on the law" because they have exceeded the 12-hour time limit of the federal Hours of Service Act and consequently may not continue any railroad operations. Also, to be outlawed.

DINGER: Yardmaster.

DIVISION: (1) That portion of a railroad assigned to the supervision of an officer called a *superintendent;* (2) The labor union local of the Brotherhood of Locomotive Engineers.

DOUBLE, TO: (1) To take a train in two separate movements over a stretch of track, usually an upgrade; (2) To work two consecutive runs in a row without rest in between; (3) To move cars of a *cut* on one track to a cut of cars on another track.

DRAG: A slow freight, often consisting of empty or mineral cars, heavy in relation to the locomotive power provided for it.

DRIVERS: Powered wheels of a locomotive.

DYNAMIC BRAKE: A locomotive braking system using an electrical means to convert some of the locomotive momentum into heat, thereby providing a retarding force within certain upper and lower speed limits.

DYNAMITER: A car with defective air brake equipment causing the car and the entire train to go into emergency application of brakes during a routine *reduction.*

ENGINE: In railroading, another word for locomotive and for the internal combustion engine. In this book, restricted to the latter use to avoid confusion.

ENGINEMAN: A standard and the original term for locomotive engineer, but includes locomotive fireman in some uses. Originally, an engineman operated a stationary steam engine, before the advent of locomotive steam engines.

ENGINE SERVICE: Work connected with the operation of locomotives, by engineers, firemen, and hostlers.

EXTRA BOARD: A rotating working list in which employees go to the bottom of the list when they register off duty. Extra board employees protect vacant and special assignments for a particular craft. Hours of work are at any (unpredictable) time or day.

EXTRA (train): A train not authorized by timetable schedule.

EYE: Color light indication of a block or interlocking signal.

FLAG: An assumed name.

FLAGMAN: Any railroad employee who protects train, track, or right-of-way structures with signal lights, flags, *torpedoes,* and *fusees* in accordance with flagging rule 99, or another rule.

FUSEE: A signal flare; red for stop signals or yellow for general signaling—over distances greater than can be covered by a lantern.

GANDY DANCER: Track worker.

GATE: Track switch.

GO IN THE HOLE, TO: To take a *siding* in order to *meet* or be *passed* by another *train,* or for another purpose.

GRAB IRONS: Hand railings on cars used for hand hold when mounting, dismounting, or riding on the side of a car.

GROUNDMAN: Operating employee in *train* or *yard service.*

GUN: *Torpedo.*

HAND BRAKE: A brake system on each piece of *rolling stock* activated by human muscle power where the turning of a wheel or pumping of a lever activates mechanical devices which apply brakes to wheel tread or to axle-mounted braking disc.

HIGHBALL: Hand or oral signal to move a train, in accordance with any restrictive rules.

HIGH IRON: Main line, laid with heavier (and higher) rail than other tracks.

HOG: Any locomotive. Originally, a consolidation-type steam locomotive originating before the turn of the century.

HOGHEAD: A locomotive engineer. Also, hogger and eagle-eye.

HOME SIGNAL: A wayside *block* or *interlocking signal* that governs movement into a route or *block.*

HOTBOX: Overheated *journal,* which can lock or break an axle, resulting in derailment.

INDEPENDENT BRAKES: Locomotive brake system applying brakes by direct introduction of compressed air into brake cylinders.

INTERLOCKING: An arrangement of wayside signals and other appliances (such as track switches and *derails*) so interconnected that conflicting movements at railraod crossings, junctions, and other places may not be lined up by the interlocking operator, at his central control station, such as a tower. Interlocking signals are of the same general appearance as the three types of *block signals.*

JOIN THE BIRDS, TO: To jump from a moving piece of *rolling stock,* usually just before a wreck.

JOURNAL: Axle bearing on *rolling stock.*

KICK, TO: To propel one or more freight cars only at a velocity allowing uncoupled movement into classification tracks, once locomotive speed is reduced.

LOCAL: A freight which sets out, picks up, and switches cars throughout an assigned area or district, for example, a stretch of main line, a branch line, or an industrial complex outside of yard limits. With the addition of running over main track, local ground crews work in a manner similar to yard/terminal area switchmen. Certain through-freight trains may be assigned duties of a local. Also, way-freight and peddler.

LUNG: Drawbar, steel shank supporting a *coupler*.

MARKER: A red or green light or a combination of these or other prescribed signal (such as a flag or reflectorized disc) affixed to the rear end of *rolling stock* operated as a *train*.

MEET: The going by one another of two trains moving in opposite directions on *single track*. One train must necessarily be in the clear on a *siding* in order to prevent a "cornfield meet," or head-on collision.

MUDHOP: Yard clerk.

NONOP: Railroad nonoperating personnel, including mechanical forces, maintenance-of-way forces, and many clerical positions.

NO-BILL: (1) Nonunion employee; (2) A car for which no bill/information is available.

ON THE CARPET: Being subject to an official investigation.

ON THE GROUND: Derailed rolling stock.

OP: Railroad operating personnel, having to do with the movement of trains and other rolling stock, includes all in *engine, train,* and *yard* service, plus train dispatchers, telegraph operators, and yardmasters.

PASS: The going by one another of two trains moving in the same direction on double or *single track:* One train must necessarily be in the clear on a *siding*.

PASSING TRACK: See siding.

PIGGYBACK: Transportation of containers or highway trailers on flat cars. Also, TOFC and COFC.

PILOT: (1) Generally smooth-surfaced steel, protective barrier at lower front of steam locomotive and front and rear of a diesel; (2) An operating employee assigned to a train whose engineer or conductor is not familiar with rules or right-of-way for district over which they will operate.

PLUG IT, TO: To put *automatic brake* system into emergency application. Also, to wipe the clock.

PULL THE PIN, TO: (1) To uncouple a piece of rolling stock by pulling up the coupler pin; (2) To resign from employment with a railroad.

RAIL: (1) An operating railroader; (2) One of a pair of parallel steel bars resting upon crossties of a railroad track and spiked 4 feet 8 and ½ inches apart.

RAWHIDE, TO: When a person causes someone to perform extra work, or work in a manner more difficult than required.

REDUCTION: A decreasing of the brake pipe pressure in the *automatic brake* system for the purpose of applying such brakes.

REEFER: Refrigerator car.

REGULAR TRAIN: A *train* authorized by operating timetable schedule.

ROAD: Main (line) track.

ROAD FOREMAN OF ENGINES: Formerly a Mechanical Department supervisor of engine service employees, but now an Operating Department officer, ranking in a limbo somewhere below a trainmaster, with supervisory duties involving train and locomotive handling and operating rules.

ROCKING CHAIR: Pension.

ROLL BY: An inspection for defects of a train which is rolling past one's mobile or stationary workplace.

ROLLING STOCK: Wheeled equipment used on railroad track, including locomotives, freight and passenger cars, self-propelled passenger cars and cranes, plows, and other flanged wheeled equipment.

SANDHOUSE, TO: To chat about railroad operations or the personal behavior or characteristics of another railroader.

SCHEDULE: That part of an operating *timetable* which prescribes class, direction, number, and route for a regular train; for example, westward First Class No. 5 via secondary main line A to F and then Chicago main line F to Z.

SECTION: One of two or more *regular trains* running on the same *schedule* displaying green train signals or for which such signals are displayed.

SHOOFLY: Temporary bypass track, usually around damaged or obstructed track or track under repair.

SIDING: A track auxiliary to the main track for meeting or passing trains. Also, passing track.

SINGLE TRACK: A main track in which trains are operated in both directions.

SPOT, TO: To position a piece of *rolling stock* where required for loading, unloading, or working upon it. "To go on spot" is to stop working for a while and rest.

SPUR: A track with only one turnout (switch) leading to a nonspur track.

STAB, TO: To delay a *train* other than one's own.

STATION: A place designated in the *timetable* by name. No depot or other building need be present at a named (Ajax) or numbered (Spur 3) station.

STUDENT: Officially, an operating trainee during a designated period of initial learning of an operating craft. Actually, a term for any *op,* operating employee, in the first year or so in railroading.

SUPERINTENDENT: The supreme manager of all operating and nonoperating personnel and their work on a *division* of a railroad.

SUPERIOR TRAIN: A *train* having precedence over another train. Superiority may be by right (conferred by *train order*), by class, and by direction (both conferred by operating *timetable*). Right is superior to class or direction. Direction is superior between *regular trains* of the same class, but not between *extra trains*. Regular trains are superior to extra trains, first class trains to second class, and so forth, and preceding *sections* of a *schedule* are superior to the succeeding ones.

TIE DOWN, TO: To set *hand brakes* on *rolling stock.*

TIMETABLE, OPERATING: The authority governing movement of *trains* subject to the rules. It contains classified *schedules* of *regular trains;* classified lists of all *stations* with coded indication of facilities, kind of track, and signals, if any, at that point; and special operating, air brake, and other rules and instructions. (Public timetables contain classified schedules of passenger trains for passenger stations only and some information for passengers.)

TORPEDO: A rail-mounted explosive cap, giving a sharp and loud report when run over by *rolling stock.* Used for audible signals in accordance with the rules.

TRAIN: A locomotive, or locomotives coupled, with or without cars displaying a *marker* or markers.

TRAIN LINE: See brake pipe.

TRAINMASTER: An operating officer who supervises a part of a *division* or a terminal of a division.

TRAIN ORDER: Instructions issued in writing by dispatcher in prescribed forms on a standard tissue paper blank in accordance with train order rules for movement of trains not provided for by *timetable* schedule or other authority.

TRAIN SERVICE: Nonengine service work connected with handling of trains and cars outside of yard limits, by conductors and brakemen.

TRUCK: (On *rolling stock*) a heavy flexible steel frame holding *journals* attached to wheel-axle assemblies and containing components of air brake equipment and heavy springs. The entire truck rotates against underframe of rolling stock by means of a heavy steel pin.

UNIT: A complete single diesel-electric or electric locomotive, usually capable of being operated in multiple with other units from one workspace as a multiple-unit locomotive.

VARNISH: Passenger train, from the days of varnished wooden cars.

WABASH, TO: To sideswipe rolling stock. Also, to corner.

WASHOUT: Violent hand stop signal.

WHISKERS: A considerable amount of seniority in a craft on a district.

WOODEN-AXLE RAILROAD: A substandard carrier characterized by poor maintenance of rolling stock and right-of-way and by operations of less than average quality.

WORK TRAIN: A train carrying materials and equipment for maintenance or construction of track or other parts of right-of-way. Designated as a work *extra* train.

Case Studies in Contemporary American Culture, from Case Studies in Cultural Anthropology and Case Studies in Education and Culture, edited by George and Louise Spindler.

Aschenbrenner, Joyce LIFELINES: Black Families in Chicago
Individual and family networks in an urban setting
1975/160 **Pages/ISBN:** 0-03-012826-9

Collier, John, Jr. ALASKAN ESKIMO EDUCATION: A Film Analysis of Cultural Confrontation in the Schools (CSEC)
Classrooms in BIA schools; confrontation of Angle and Eskimo cultures.
1973/130 **Pages/ISBN:** 0-03-088021-1

Daner, Francine Jeanne, THE AMERICAN CHILDREN OF KRSNA
A study of a contemporary alternative religion based on participant observation.
1976/128 **Pages/ISBN:** 0-03-013546-X

Davidson, R. Theodore CHICANO PRISONERS: The Key to San Quentin
Prison culture from perspective of the Family; the Baby Mafia.
1974/196 **Pages/ISBN:** 0-03-091616-X

Dougherty, Molly Crocker BECOMING A WOMAN IN RURAL BLACK CULTURE
A modified community study focusing on the social maturation of black adolescent girls in rural north Florida.
1978/128 **Pages/ISBN:**0-03-014921-5

Friedland, William H./Nelkin, Dorothy MIGRANT: Agricultural Workers in America's Northeast
Work crew and its control, relationship with the outside world.
1971/281 **Pages/ISBN:** 0-03-085767-8

Hicks, George L. APPALACHIAN VALLEY
Culturally distinctive folk culture of the Appalachians.
1976/128 **Pages/ISBN:** 0-03-077305-9

Hostetler, John A./Huntington, Gertrude E. CHILDREN IN AMISH SOCIETY: Socialization and Community Education (CSEC)
Amish school and community versus the outside world.
1971/119 **Pages/ISBN:** 0-03-077750-X

Hostetler, John A./Huntington, Gertrude E. THE HUTTERITES IN NORTH AMERICA
World view, technology, family and socialization, communal organization. New Fieldwork Edition
1979/119 **Pages/ISBN:** 0-03-065005-4

Jacobs, Jerry FUN CITY: An Ethnographic Study of A Retirement Community
An "active way of life" is designed but only a few participate.
1974/96 Pages/ISBN: 0-03-001936-2

*Keiser, R. Lincoln THE VICE LORDS: Warriors of the Streets
Gang membership, territoriality, leadership in Chicago. New fieldwork edition.
1979/96 Pages/ISBN:0-03-045396-8

Madsen William THE MEXICAN-AMERICANS OF SOUTH TEXAS, Second
Edition
Anglo-American relations, class differences, folk beliefs, and acculturation. New edition with epilogue by Andre Guerrero.
1973/124 Pages/ISBN: 0-03-008431-8

McFee, Malcolm MODERN BLACKFEET: Montanans on a Reservation
Indian-oriented and white-oriented adaptations. Why assimilation has not occurred.
1972/134 Pages/ISBN: 0-03-085768-6

O'Toole, James WATTS AND WOODSTOCK: Identity and Culture in the
United States and South Africa
Comparison of Watts, Los Angeles, and Woodstock, a Coloured ghetto in Cape
Twon.
1972/154 Pages/ISBN: 0-03-000936-7

Partridge, William L. THE HIPPIE GHETTO: The Natural History of a Subculture
Rituals, values, and sentiments; as a revitalization movement, not a counter culture.
1972/88 Pages/ISBN: 0-03-091081-1

Pilcher, William W. THE PORTLAND LONGSHOREMEN: A Dispersed
Urban Community
Work culture, extra-work activities, union, family, and race relations.
1972/128 Pages/ISBN: 0-03-091289-X

Rosenfeld, Gerry "SHUT THOSE THICK LIPS!": A Study of Slum School Failure (CSEC)
Why and how inner city schools fail. The network of self-sustaining perceptions.
1971/120 Pages/ISBN: 0-03-085350-8

Spindler, George/Spindler, Louise URBAN ANTHROPOLOGY IN THE U.S.
A collection of case studies designed to give students exposure to four major segments of American urban Society—*Chicano Prisoners: The Key to San Quentin, Lifelines: Black Families in Chicago, Fun City: An Ethnographic Study of a Retirement Community, Portland Longshoremen: A Dispersed Urban Community.*

Spindler, George/Spindler, Louise DREAMERS WITHOUT POWER: The
Menomini Indians
Cognitive organization and adaptive strategies to the confrontation with Anglo-American culture and power in five contemporary groups.
1971/208 Pages/ISBN: 0-03-085542-X

Spindler, George/Spindler, Louise **NATIVE NORTH AMERICANS: Four Cases**
Four previously published CSCA covering most important culture areas of native
North America—*Hano: A Tewa Indian Community in Arizona; The Kwakiutl: Indians
of British Columbia; Modern Blackfeet; Montanans on a Reservation; The Menominee.*
1977/512 **Pages/ISBN: 0-03-018401-0**

Sugarman, Barry **DAYTOP VILLAGE: A Therapeutic Community**
Resocialization and values in a well-known drug rehabilitation center.
1974/134 **Pages/ISBN: 0-03-086291-4**

*Ward, Martha C. **THEM CHILDREN: A Study in Language Learning (CSEC)**
How children in a small black Louisiana community acquire speech.
1971/99 **Pages/ISBN: 0-03-086294-9**

Wolcott, Harry F. **THE MAN IN THE PRINCIPAL'S OFFICE: An Ethnography (CSEC)**
Ethnography of middle class elementary school and principal. Shows how principal
acts as mediator and system-supporter.
1973/334 **Pages/ISBN: 0-03-091236-9**

*Out of print, but available in most libraries.